# THE DAVE TEST

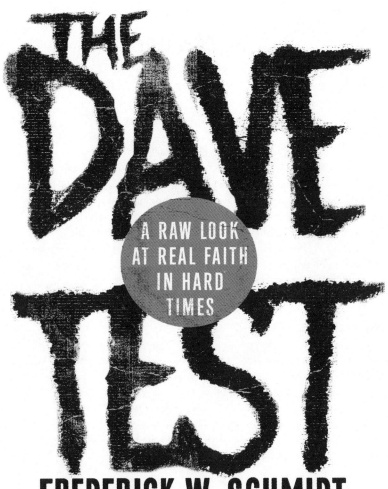

# THE DAVE TEST

A RAW LOOK AT REAL FAITH IN HARD TIMES

## FREDERICK W. SCHMIDT

**Abingdon Press**

Nashville

# THE DAVE TEST
## A Raw Look at Real Faith in Hard Times

**Library of Congress Cataloging-in-Publication Data has been requested.**

ISBN 978-1-4267-5593-4

13 14 15 16 17 18 19 20 21 22—10 9 8 7 6 5 4 3 2 1
MANUFACTURED IN THE UNITED STATES OF AMERICA

For David Mark Schmidt, M.D.,
my brother

# CONTENTS

# CONTENTS

# FOREWORD

FRED SCHMIDT IS A THOUGHTFUL, COMPELLING, insightful theologian who has done all the necessary homework of his craft. But that is not what interests us here. What interests us here is that Fred has a brother. His name is Dave. He was surgeon. He had a brain tumor that finally killed him. Fred, in what is given to us here, is deeply engaged with his brother, Dave, in being with him, in being with him in his walk to death, in reflecting on and learning from that companionship of candor and loss.

The title of the book, *The Dave Test*, refers to a set of questions that have emerged from and shaped that intense companionship and its work. They are questions about getting real and being truthful with the wretchedness of death and loss. To pass the Dave Test is to face reality, loss, and grief without denial

or phoniness or cover-up, to face it in all of its uncompromis-
ing demand. The chapters of this small but important book
are reflections, one at a time, on the questions that constitute
the Dave Test. What comes through here is mature faith that is
shaped, informed, and judged by this deep love for a brother
who majored in honesty and who for that reason eschewed all
the phoniness that passes for care and faith and hope among us.

It strikes me that what Fred outlines here is a concrete
embodiment of the drama of the book of Job. That sufferer was
famously caught between the reality of loss that could not be
denied and the easy, conventional explanations offered by the
"friends" who voice the settled conventions of faith who are,
in fact, not interested in the bodily reality on the ground. The
work of the book of Job is an adjudication of that tension been
the lived reality and the explanatory conventions. Job refused
to lie or to yield, even when caught up by the tsunami of the
creator God.

Fred sees himself and especially Dave in the same contes-
tation. Only here it is not the rigor of self-assured covenantal
rigidity of Job's companions. It is, rather, well-meaning friends
and their practice of reassurance. The pseudo-faith they medi-
ate is a practice of denial that wants to explain away the bodily
reality that is in front of them. As a result the church, in this
reading, stands exposed by its clichés, it certitudes, and its
easy assurances that are popularly mouthed among us. But of
course it is not simply the church; the same practice of denial
permeates popular culture and its assumed well-being that can
be generated by the chase of some commodity that may take

many forms. But all such commodity solutions are designed to conceal bodily reality; in that much-repeated portrayal, everyone is happy, everyone is young, everyone is in good health or soon can be by a procedure or a product, world without end! I suppose it is no surprise that the church is tempted to imitate such a seductive culture.

In the end, however, Fred's presentation is not primarily concerned to indict church or culture. It is rather to share with us in quite concrete form what he has learned that could make a difference as we walk with other sisters and brothers who face such loss. He has learned what is always again to be relearned, because it is so contradictory of our common propensity and our usual practice. Friends that effectively stand by Dave love freely; acknowledge their own mortality and so need not be Promethean in their manner; are available to those in need, to God, and to themselves; are vulnerable, and speak with candor. Of course! But it is so hard! It turns out that this lived reality, reported here with such poignancy, is the core wisdom of our faith tradition:

-That **truth makes free**...not happy, not easy, not successful, but free!

-That **perfect love casts out fear**...well, maybe not all fear, but most of it. Dave is less fearful with Fred there!

The book is an uncommon account of what our society does not want to know and cannot remember, but what we need to know in bodily ways if we are to live the life and die the death that is given to us.

I read this book with great attentiveness because it rings true. More than that, I read it with great attentiveness because I also have a brother, Ed. Ed lives with kidney failure, and his doctors have given him a limited time for his life. Ed, moreover, is like Dave, no bull-shitter. He can spot a phony a mile away. He is rooted in faith, but he is totally impatient with phoniness. For me every reference to Dave sounded like Ed, and I can see myself in Fred's place. But then, every reader who pays attention will make something of a like identity as stand-in for Fred with some Dave who is at risk.

This book will be cherished. Because all of us, like Fred and Dave, face loss. We are never ready, I imagine. And we have no resources for that except ourselves, framed as we variously are, by our narratives of faith and unfaith, of compelling truth and fulsome denial. We may be grateful for Fred's self-giving to Dave and for Dave's relentless honesty. The truth of our life does not come in explanation. It comes in presence! In the end Fred finishes with *faith* and with *loneliness*; perhaps the two come together:

"I am utterly dependent upon the One who loves us both and am grateful in ways that escape expression. But, oh, how I miss him."

Final words for final loss!

Walter Brueggemann
Columbia Theological Seminary

July 17, 2013

# INTRODUCTION

"GOD, HELP ME, WHERE DO YOU START?"

That was the plea an old friend from high school posted on Facebook a few weeks after his sister's death. She was forty-eight years old.

Where *do* we start? How do we care for ourselves and for one another when life... well, when life just sucks?

When jobs or life-giving relationships end?
When a physician says that we have weeks or months
    to live?
When a child dies?
When an illness or a handicap forces us to live around
    its demands and limitations?

Those questions have dogged me for years and for a lot of reasons. Some of them are personal. Some of them are professional. I am an Episcopal priest. People expect clergy like me to know what to say in awful situations. But we don't always know. Sometimes we don't have a clue what to say.

Recently that quest for what to say in bad situations acquired new urgency. Seven years ago I learned that my brother, Dave, has cancer. He has not just any kind of cancer but life-ending cancer—the kind that guts your life, leaves you with nothing, and *then* kills you.

Dave is also a Christian. So initially he looked to the church for answers to the "God-help-me-where-do-you-start" question. That isn't surprising. He is a Baptist, and going to church runs deep in Baptist bones.

But Dave doesn't go to church anymore. The church really doesn't speak to his life.

He explains it this way:

If the preacher isn't using stained-glass language that I can't pin down and apply to my life, then instead he is blowing sunshine up my ass, telling me the whole experience is a blessing in disguise.

I'm a fifty-something hand surgeon. I operated on 120 patients a month until I discovered that I have brain cancer. I have a glioblastoma grade four tumor. All but 3 percent of the people who have this type of tumor are dead within a year.

What in hell am I going to do with my life that is going
to be more of a blessing to other people than what I
was doing?

It's hard, he points out, when you've been told that you have a
brain tumor to hear people tell you that "God has a plan," that
"the best is yet to come," or that God is giving you "a blessing
in disguise." When you say that to someone who has a tumor
that claims the lives of all but 3 percent of those who have them
within a year, the words are worse than useless.

It's no surprise, then, that the two friends he has who speak
most readily and directly to him about the spiritual demands of
life are no-nonsense, plainspoken recovering alcoholics. They
lack the churchy, theological vocabulary of a priest or pastor.
They haven't studied the Scriptures in any formal sense of the
word, and they don't go to church.

What they have done is sharpen what they believe, testing the shape of their spiritual convictions against the hard
realities of life. They care for one another, face the truth, tell the
truth, and look for truth that they can hold on to.

"The institutional crap doesn't mean anything to them,"
my brother observes.

Both men—and others whom I have met—are people who
pass what I've started calling *the Dave Test.*

The Dave Test is a set of ten questions you can ask yourself
when life sucks or before you talk to someone whose life is in
the same sort of place. It is a test that will keep you from

Thinking and saying hurtful things
Looking for comfort at the expense of others
Using stained-glass language
Defending broken ideas about God

It is a test that will keep you

Honest about just how harrowing life can be
Present to your friends
In touch with God

What we are told and what we say to others when life goes to hell can be crushing or comforting. It can ring true, or it can sound like a pack of lies. If you are looking for God, honesty, answers, direction, and peace (or if you are trying to help others find them), then apply the Dave Test before you open your mouth or believe what you are told. No flinching, squinting, or sugarcoating the truth.

Each chapter of this book is devoted to one of the ten Dave Test questions:

Can I say, "Life sucks"?
Can I give up my broken gods?
Can I avoid using stained-glass language?
Can I admit that some things will never get better?
Can I give up trading in magic and superstition?
Can I stop blowing smoke?
Can I say something that helps?
Can I grieve with others?
Can I walk wounded?
Can I be a friend?

In each chapter I tackle one of those ten questions, offering some thoughts about how you might find your own, more durable answers and deeper ways of living and exploring answers that might be misleading or hurtful.

I invite you to use the Dave Test not just to examine the value of what you think, do, and say. I urge you to use the questions to craft a different way of living and caring for yourself and for others.

The Dave Test is not a method. No one ever saved a friend by arming oneself with the right answers or by making compassionate noises. What we need when we suffer are companions who are, by nature, able to walk with us and love us. Each of those people will look a bit different. Some of them will look *very* different from what you might expect.

When I shared an earlier draft of this introduction with Dave, he sent it along to one of his friends who wrote back:

> Thanks, buddy! It reads well and is embarrassingly kind toward your two asshole friends. Doesn't he know how we laughed when you fell in the lake in Canada? . . . Yes, he mentions going to the shooting range, but why doesn't he mention that we comment that you can't see for shit? . . . P.S. Where are you? Are you and your truck available on Friday afternoon? And don't give me shit about being out of town or not feeling well. This is all about me.

There is no prescription for caring this way, and this version of caring might not be your cup of tea (or bottle of beer).

You may not like the language or this kind of humor. For example, my wife would not talk to her friends the same way that some guys talk to one another.

That's not the point. You don't need to use the language of Dave's friend's e-mail as your model. Here's what happened:

> Dave's friend acknowledged Dave's illness and its difficulties.
> He treated Dave like a whole human being who didn't need to be coddled or pitied.
> He used humor.
> He talked to Dave like an adult whom he still expected to function in the world.
> And he gave Dave a job, even if it was just lending Dave's pickup truck to a friend.

There were other things that didn't happen:

> My brother's friend didn't try to make himself comfortable at Dave's expense by minimizing his struggle.
> He didn't assume a faintly tragic tone and try to make Dave a project or a charity case.
> And he didn't try to make himself feel good at Dave's expense by somehow calling attention to "what a really good friend he has been."

That's a lot to accomplish in the few lines of an e-mail message, but it's all there and captures the goal of this book. *The Dave Test* is designed to start us on that journey of becoming our own versions of people who care: people who can be themselves, who have found a new place to sit with their own suffering, and who can walk with friends in the hardest of times.

This journey is about soul craft. It's about growing up and about becoming fully alive, fully human, and completely available to the people we love.

Suffering and sorrow are not things God sends our way, but they can and do radicalize life. We can allow that radicalization to grow within us. We can let it change, deepen, and ennoble us. Or we can run from the challenge it presents. But if we do run, then we will live our lives in hiding—hiding from ourselves, from one another, from life's realities, and from God.

My hope is that this book will provide a place to do the kind of soul work that will spare us that experience and enrich our shared journey.

# QUESTION ONE:
## CAN I SAY, "LIFE SUCKS"?

# QUESTION ONE:
## CAN I SAY, "LIFE SUCKS"?

"THAT SUCKS." CAN YOU EVEN GET THOSE WORDS out of your mouth? A lot of us can't. There was a time when I couldn't.

The language isn't the issue, of course. It's the struggle to be honest about just how hard and ugly life can be.

When Dave was diagnosed with brain cancer, he was operating on 120 patients a month. One of Nashville's go-to guys for hand surgery, he had just finished a long day of work in the operating room, and, as he was washing his hands, he experienced what his physicians later described as a "visual seizure."

Suddenly, all he could see were images from earlier in the day and the surgeries he had just completed. He couldn't see his hands, the washbasin, the water, or the soap dispenser.

3

The experience didn't last long that first time, so he didn't think much of it. It had been a long day. He was operating on a lot of people. The surgeries were visually demanding, requiring the use of lasers and microscopes. There was every reason to chalk the experience up to eyestrain, and he was going on vacation the next day anyway.

But he was less sure that was the case when, in the middle of the following week, the same thing happened again. He was halfway through a run down the beach one morning of his vacation, and all he could see were images from earlier in the day. He couldn't see his feet, his hands, or the sand beneath him. Worse yet, this time the episode lasted longer.

So, on his return home he contacted a friend of his who is a neurosurgeon. "Bob, I think I need an MRI." Bob obliged, and shortly after the test was completed he had the results in hand.

"Dave, I think that I've discovered the problem. There is a mass pressing against the occipital lobe of your brain, and because it's the sight center, the mass is frustrating your brain's efforts to process images from the optic nerve. So you are getting the neural equivalent of delayed feedback."

In that moment Dave's medical career came to end. He knew that he could no longer safely operate or practice medicine. He informed the chief of surgery, and he hasn't been able to work a day since. Then he made plans to have his head cut open.

Call it what you will, that sucks. It sucks for Dave. It sucks for his family. It sucks for the people he might have helped with his knowledge and skills.

But there were a limited number of people in Dave's circle of friends who were willing to acknowledge that things were that bad. Most of his friends and particularly his friends at church said things like, "It's a blessing in disguise, Dave," or, "God's got something bigger for you out there."

Not surprising, Dave doesn't find that kind of language helpful at all. In fact, it drove him away from church and pared down his friendships to a handful of intimate relationships.

The impulse to say comforting things when someone we know gets a terrible diagnosis is understandable. We want to find some way of supporting people and making them feel better when they receive gut-wrenching and life-changing news. But there are better ways of doing that than uttering banal, even false, platitudes.

What did Dave need that he wasn't getting from his church? Or, put more positively, what can we do for one another under such circumstances?

**We can demonstrate our love for others in the painful place that life has put them.** When we can't bring ourselves to say, "That sucks," when life really does suck, we fail to love others where they are and as they are. Instead we force those who are suffering to amend their understanding of what has happened to them as a precondition of being loved.

"Cheer up."

"Look on the bright side."

"It could have been worse."

"Don't be so negative."

When we say those false, cheery things to suffering people, they run. They tell us as little as possible about their struggles, or they tell us what they think we want to hear. How many times have you heard this exchange when it can't possibly be true?

Question directed to someone who is plainly suffering: "How are you?"

Response from the person who is suffering (and who knows the person asking the question is not going to be able to say, "That sucks"): "Oh, I'm fine." (Unspoken thought: "FINE, which is an acronym for Freaked out, Insecure, Neurotic, and Emotional, but I don't trust you enough to tell you.")

I've been there. I've used that response. Anyone who belongs to the fellowship of the suffering has used it.

"Oh, I'm fine."

I reserve the word *fine* for people who don't really care, for people who don't really want to know how things are, for people who are clueless, for people who are going to dispense Hallmark wisdom, and especially for people who want me to change as a precondition of love.

To be sure, there are times when we need to change the way that we think about a tragedy or loss. Even irreparable losses require more reflection than is possible at first—if life gives us enough time to reflect, that is.

When we first receive tragic news, we often panic. We allow fear to overwhelm us, and we lose perspective. We can be obsessed with choices that might have yielded a different result. We can be strangled by what lies ahead. Or we can be paralyzed by a combination of both fear of the past and dread of the future. Rightly, I had a spiritual director years ago who pointed out, "If you have one foot in the past and another in the future, you shit on the present."

But in a lot of cases—and certainly in Dave's case—there is no "other way" to think about loss, not in any way that changes the fact that he is dying. And even if there were changes he could make, he can't start there, and neither could we.

> You were a surgeon. Now you are not.
> You were a contributor. Now you are not.
> You were on a journey. Now you are at a dead end.
> You weren't going to live forever. Now you aren't going to live long at all.
> You were going to watch your children grow up. Now you aren't.
> You were going to have grandchildren. Now you will never see them.

When you think about it, frankly, it's stunning how much loss people are prepared to sweep aside for their own emotional security with the words, "It's a blessing in disguise."

When life has gone to hell, we need to feel the loss. We need to register it. We need to test the weight of the experience if we are going to get an accurate assessment of what we've lost or where we are. And, eventually, we need to "re-learn the world"—if we have time (we don't always).[1]

We can't begin to re-learn the world until we've been loved where we are and have been given the space to feel the loss.

Most of us can't do that adequately without people who are willing to say to us, "Man, this is bad. It's really bad. Let me sit here among the ashes with you. Let me survey the destruction with you"—not as resident experts or know-it-alls who have all the answers, but as people who love us enough to admit that this is hard.

To have that space—to feel loved and heard in that space— we need others to acknowledge that we are truly in a place where life sucks.

**In that space where we know that we are loved and heard we can rehearse what has happened. We can examine our wounds and we can evaluate what the losses really are.** No physician would try to treat a patient's wounds without an examination and no one who grieves can re-learn the world without first unpacking the implications of the losses one has suffered.

When Dave went to medical school, he was not just preparing for a career in medicine. He was on a journey of self-discovery.

My father dominated our home, and—thanks to his own insecurities—he dominated everyone around him. He had convictions about what was and was not worth doing in life. He had plans for us. To make matters worse, when we weren't appreciative in the way he expected or when we deviated from his plan, he showed it in ways that were loud and violent.

As a result, when Dave went off to medical school, he wasn't looking just for a place to make a living; he was looking for a world that he could call his own—a place where he could achieve his own goals and chart his own course.

The cancer his physicians discovered was the presenting cause of his grief. But the deeper losses were the things that disappeared in the wake of his illness: the world he had crafted, the ways in which he had helped others, his sense of personal worth, and his identity as a physician.

Behind every loss is not just the trauma of the event alone—divorce, unemployment, a fatal diagnosis—there are also what grief counselors call the inevitable "secondary" losses. The problem, of course, is that the word *secondary* is completely misleading. The consequences of a tragedy may be "secondary" in time, but these are the deeper losses, and they are not always evident at first glance:

- Divorce is difficult, but it may rob us of the certainty that we are loved. It certainly robs us of our dreams for the future.
- Unemployment is hard. What is hardest is the way it deprives us of a sense of security, control, and independence.
- Illness may rob us of hope or of a means of actively connecting with life around us.
- Sexual assault may rob us of that ineffable quality we call "innocence" and the ability to trust that the world is not always a malevolent place.
- In Dave's case, illness robbed him of a life that was all his own. It robbed him of the life he had created.

What you offer a suffering friend when you honestly say, "That sucks," is the space in which your friend can name her losses. Dave needed months to name what he had lost, and in the absence of a place to explore those losses, it would have taken longer. But he had a few friends who gave him the space to do that. In a word, we need people who can love us when we suffer *and* can give us space where we can register and explore our loss.

**We also need witnesses to our pain, loss, and grief.** Therein lies the difference between love that demands we change first and "get past" all that grief stuff and love that begins by accepting us where we are. The notion of witnessing to someone else's loss, pain, or grief may seem pretty abstract and even unnecessary. The most familiar associations most of us have with "witnesses," "witnessing," and "testimony" are tied to the courtroom or the church. We talk about witnessing or giving testimony for the benefit of a jury regarding events that others may not have seen, or we talk about the religious obligation to tell people what God has been doing in our lives.

But witnessing can have an even more primal place in our lives: witnessing on behalf of someone whose life is in the pit is saying out loud that you have seen that person struggle. It is saying that what that person is experiencing is hard or unfair. It is also witnessing to that which is otherwise unseen—sometimes even to the one who suffers.[2]

To talk about suffering as "unseen" may sound like nonsense, since we are all surrounded by people who "see" us struggle on a daily basis. There are doctors, nurses, fellow employees, relatives, friends, neighbors, and others who are simply around at the time. Of course they *see* what is happening—or so we think.

But witnessing to the suffering of another is not that simple, and there is a lot that is missed in that kind of seeing. For one thing, the experience of suffering is itself isolating and hides a great deal from us as witnesses. Dave spends countless hours in relative isolation, taking intravenous chemotherapy drugs. Every month he lays in a long, coffinlike tube for a regular MRI. He is essentially alone when he does these things.

Even the people who administer those tests and drugs do not experience what Dave goes through. They probe his body with a needle, looking for a place to administer his drugs, but they have no idea what it is like to be subjected to that experience. Much of what they "see" is seen at arm's length, emotionally and physically.

The effect that both the cancer and the treatments have had on Dave's sight visually separates him from the world outside. He can only see half of what is in front of him, and he constantly scans his surroundings by turning his head. Half of the world is always missing thanks to the damage done to the sight center of his brain.

Seizures, too, cut him off from his surroundings, making it impossible for him to connect with the world around him in a natural, fluid fashion. "Chemo-brain"—the fog-inducing effect that chemotherapy drugs have on the cognitive process—deepens that effect, giving him the sense that he is "swimming in cotton."

Some of that suffering is not "seen" at all, and there is a feeling of "aloneness" when those who love you cannot share those experiences. Navigate the world without hearing or without seeing everything around you—hammer your brain in ways that rob you of speed and acuity—and you begin to experience the world in ways that are forever changed.

That is not just true of cancer victims. It is true for the divorced, the unemployed, and the physically impaired. It is true for people whose children become addicted to drugs. It is true for women who suffer domestic abuse. It is true for many people in prison.

**Even if all of that suffering were "seen," there is still a huge difference between having someone see you struggle and having someone say that he or she has seen you struggle.** When we are "isolated," as the Latin origin of the word suggests, we are "an island." We are cut off and surrounded by barriers that make contact with others impossible.

To suffer is to be isolated. In fact, there is even physiological evidence to suggest that isolation changes the white matter of our brains, disrupting normal brain function.[3] So, the isolating nature of suffering is not just a metaphor for a spiritual and emotional experience. It is not just about a loss of relationships with other people and with the world around us. It has physical dimensions as well.

To say, "That sucks," is to register or recognize just how bad things are for someone else. To witness to suffering—to say that we have seen it—is to reach into the isolation, whether we share in it or not.

When that happens, whether the unseen struggle is the aftermath of divorce, the loss of employment, a life-destroying illness, or a crippling injury, that kind of witness has an unexpected power to liberate someone who is isolated.

- It eases the loneliness.
- It has the power to break the isolation that the one who suffers feels.
- It has the power to name kinds of isolation and loss that the one who suffers may labor with but not yet recognize.
- It has the power to encourage, whether the suffering has a solution or not.
- It has the power to free someone to claim the dignity that rightly belongs to that person in the middle of a struggle that may be unrelenting.

Just how a lived witness to pain and loss can make that kind of difference is difficult to describe. There are the inevitably human dimensions of witnessing, I suppose: our need for companionship, the need to be touched (both literally and figuratively), and our need to know that someone is paying attention. I am struck by the way the conversations that Dave has with family and friends seem to lift his sense of isolation and despair, even when things have been difficult.

But I think that there is also something fundamentally spiritual about that kind of witness as well. We Christians are fond of talking about how Jesus understands our struggles.

That conviction is based on what we describe as the doctrine of the incarnation, and it is all about God taking on human flesh.

As far as Jesus is concerned, that's a one-of-a-kind event. But I'm convinced that in a very real sense, when we are prepared to sit alongside someone else and say, "That sucks," there is a sense in which we lend our own voice and presence to the work of incarnation. We are Jesus-with-flesh-on, someone who says without equivocation, "I understand that this is hard and overwhelming."

Although I understand that dynamic in distinctively Christian terms, I don't think for a moment that Christians are the only ones who can provide that witness to the suffering of others. Singer-songwriter Marc Cohn, who is Jewish, was sitting in a van with his band after a concert in Denver in 2005. An armed gunman stepped in front of the van, evidently intending to steal it, and shot Cohn in the head. A battle with post-traumatic stress and the effect that Hurricane Katrina had on New Orleans three weeks later, where his wife was serving as a reporter, prompted Cohn to write these words, which he set to music[4]:

> When your longest night is coming down
> When pieces of you hit the ground
> When every word they say about you is a lie
> When they put your soul up for review
> When they're set on turning every screw
> Call on me and I will testify
> Let me be your witness.[5]

These words suggest what we can all do for one another when "night is coming down": ease the loneliness, break the power of isolation, name the loss, encourage someone in a time of discouragement, and free someone to claim the dignity that is his or hers. That is a lot to give in the middle of an experience that may or may not have a solution.

But giving it can be as simple as being able to say, "That sucks."

# QUESTION TWO:
## CAN I GIVE UP MY BROKEN GODS?

# QUESTION TWO:
## CAN I GIVE UP MY BROKEN GODS?

WHEN YOU TELL YOUR FRIEND IN THE PIT THAT LIFE sucks, you are saying something about human experience—about your friend's human experience and perhaps about your own.

What do we say about *God* when someone admits he or she is at life's shattered edges?

Though it can be hard to know what to say about God in the midst of suffering, in fact suffering—our suffering or the suffering of another—is sometimes the very thing that invites us to let go of worn-out small ideas of God and to embrace new pictures of God, pictures that are perhaps more complex, more mature, and ultimately more sustaining.

**Where do our ideas about God come from?** In one way the answer is that there are as many sources for them as there are people. Everyone has a god or rejects a god based on one's own life experiences and a variety of influences. That's a pretty individualistic enterprise, and now, more than ever, it's not just the way we get our views of God; we are also told that it is the best way to go about getting them.[6]

However, our views of God are more caught than learned, and a lot of the learning is unconscious or subconscious. We catch our views of God from childhood and adolescent experiences of our parents, who are the first gods in our lives—or surrogates for god. We catch our views of God in churches, synagogues, mosques, and other religious or quasi-religious settings. We also catch our views of God from the culture around us, which teaches us that God is either a cosmic Santa or a hateful old man in the sky who gets his jollies by tormenting people. And we make up our minds about God based on our life experiences. Something awful or good happens, we stir in what we've been taught to expect from God, and out comes a version that corresponds with what we believe God did or didn't do.[7]

**It is no surprise, then, that when life is at its tattered edges, we offer one another all sorts of "misguided guidance" for thinking about God.** We reach back into our childhood or adolescence, grab an image of God, wrap the package in adult language, and offer it up as wisdom. We pull from the scattered lessons we were taught in our religious communities. We lean on the cultural programming that we have picked up along the way. And we draw on our own experience without ever asking whether we've interpreted it appropriately or whether our own experience is really all that representative of human experience in general.

The net result is that what people tell Dave and others who suffer is not carefully crafted theology or the product of extended reflection, meditation, and struggle. All too often the god-talk of well-meaning friends comes off like the ideas of a six-year-old or a thirteen-year-old trying to cope with the experiences of an adult armed with a grab bag of half-formed ideas about God. What Dave and a lot of us have heard or thought along the way just makes life's hard places that much harder:

- God made your life suck.
- God will make your life un-suck.
- God has a plan, and that's why your life sucks.
- God is testing you by making your life suck.
- God has something for you to learn or something for others to learn.
- God will not give you more sucky experiences than you can bear.
- You must have done something to make your life suck, and now God is punishing you.

I know I've used that phrase ("Life sucks") a lot here, and I may sound as if I am overindulging in a vulgarity. But I've used it for a reason. In part, I want you to laugh. **More to the point, I want you to note the vulgarity of the notion that this is how the experience of those who suffer can be explained.**

**Note, too, the vulgar notions of God that are implicit in those statements.**

Do we really want to say: "God wanted you to have <u>brain cancer</u> [or fill in the blank with another tragedy], so he gave you a <u>life-crushing illness and condemned you to death</u> [or fill in the blank with another appropriate set of consequences], and in the meantime he is robbing you of your capacity to help others, he is having your skull cut open and a portion of your brain scooped out, and then he is irradiating your brain and poisoning you with chemicals that might extend your life if, that is, you manage to survive the effect that the chemicals have on the healthy parts of your body"?

Or look at it from the perspective of the person who suffers. Do we really want to say: "Never mind your struggle and pain, what is the lesson you are being taught?" Do we really think that God tramples their lives so they can identify the great sin that they have committed? Do we really believe God robs people of their gifts so that they can discover the hidden mission to which they have been called? Does God really test people like a five-year-old pulling off a butterfly's wings so that he or she can find new strength to believe? Does God really stretch and twist us like little Gumby dolls to see just how much suffering we can bear before we break, fold, collapse, or die?[8]

Which is more vulgar: the phrase *life sucks* or a broken notion of God that makes God sound like a sadist? The answer is pretty clear. Frankly, ideas of that kind are far more vulgar than any phrase in the English language. As seemingly intricate as the explanations outlined above seem to be, they really represent variations on one of two simple themes: one, God caused your suffering, or, two, you sinned and caused your suffering.

**But sorting through that grab bag of God images and deciding what to keep or discard can be difficult.** Difficult enough, in fact, that most people never do it. But it is possible to find a healing vision of God that we can hold on to in times of suffering and to share that vision with those we love.

I'm going to suggest two ways of getting there. One approach involves a process of spiritual exploration and inventory. This is the do-it-yourself way of winning through to a healing vision of God.

*First, ask yourself:* when you are living at the frayed edges of life, what are the ideas about God that come to mind or get you through the struggle? (Note: Those may not be the same thing.) Do you wonder if God is punishing you? Do you think that no matter how awful the situation might be, God has a hidden purpose or blessing in mind? Be honest. The unedited truth is what we are after.

*Second, once you have identified those ideas, ask this question:* where did those ideas come from? Is your God the god of your childhood or your adolescence, or is it a god of your church or your culture? Or is your god the god of a specific moment of trauma or triumph?

This step may take some time. This is where the unconscious and subconscious may have been at work. Only time and self-examination will help you discover where these ideas entered your life. Remember, however, that this exercise is not about remembering what actually happened. Your impressions about what happened are infinitely more important than factual recollections.

*Third, once you have identified the origin of your ideas, you are ready to evaluate them.* The origin of the idea itself may tell you something. But all truth is God's truth; the origin of an idea is not the only thing that matters. Evaluating our ideas is more about asking how they fit with life, with human experience, or with the rest of what we know about God.

If you belong to a religious community, the best question to ask might be, "Does this idea fit with the rest of what my community believes about God?" This may involve drawing on the spiritual resources of your religion, including the scripture and tradition of that religion.

There are two things to remember, however. One is that every religious community has more than one name for God, and even individual communities or traditions differ over which ideas about God should be emphasized. That's partly about the complexity of God, but it's also partly about what we choose to emphasize when we talk about God. Don't assume that your community takes just one position on the subject of God and suffering. It might. Some communities can be pretty closely defined, but it's not likely.

The other thing to remember is this: the way we *think* about God often has little to do with the reality that *is* God. Often the God we reject is the God-who-isn't-necessarily-so (to coin a phrase). Humility is an essential part of the spiritual journey, and none of us understands God so thoroughly that we can claim that our god is God. In fact, the great mystics of the church have rightly argued that we can never thoroughly comprehend God in this life. That, it seems to me, is inescapable. There is an irreducible distance and difference between those of us who are created and the One who created us.

Just don't let that keep you from trying to understand. God is and can be known, even in times of suffering. Try this analogy: saying that I love my wife and that I know her is to say something about an intimate and growing relationship. It would be impossible, though, to claim that I know her so well that I can name every experience, emotion, and conviction that shapes her life. So, in other words, I know her and she is knowable. But I can't possibly claim to know her in the absolute sense of the word.

Our knowledge of God is like that, and that fact opens up endless possibilities. Our broken gods are not God, and moving beyond the broken versions of God involves opening ourselves to possibilities—many of which others have already discovered and named. You can reconsider the way in which you understand God in the midst of suffering, and, in fact, if you really want to know God, you will need to open yourself up to new possibilities. **If you don't belong to a religious community or this task seems too daunting, there is still one thing I believe that you can do: embrace the God who is prepared to suffer alongside us.**

Years ago my wife, who is also an Episcopal priest, was facilitating a retreat. One woman in attendance (let's call her

Chris) had recently lost her son in a car accident. She was heartbroken and devastated.

Understandably, Chris couldn't pray about her loss, because the broken God of her world was the one who had taken her son. So, even though she was in profound pain, she still had not completely faced her fear and sorrow, because the full measure of her loss included the sense that God had abandoned her. "God doesn't care," she said.

Wisely, my wife recommended that she tell God the truth about her feelings. So, Chris chose to lay prostrate on the chapel floor in silence that night, arms extended. As she wept and finally faced the full measure of her fear and sorrow, she felt as if she was nailed to a cross.

Then, in one of those moments that happen only when we are too tired to do anything but listen, Chris felt something touching her fingers. In a half-dream, she imagined Jesus lying alongside her on another cross. She wept, touching the fingers of Jesus, and in that moment, she knew that she wasn't alone. God had not taken her son. God shared in her sorrow.

Of all the healing visions of God, this, it seems to me, is the most powerful of all.

Dave has been treated to more than one broken god over the last seven years. Some people have been genuinely interested in helping him. Others were interested in helping themselves. Some were clearly afraid that their version of God might evaporate if they were honest about what Dave's illness said about God.

But whatever the motives, almost all of them have started in the wrong place. They have wanted to change something that is not going to change or comfort him with the prospect that it will change. They want to absolve God of responsibility for the suffering Dave has experienced. Or they want to believe for Dave and, often, for themselves that everything will work out for the best.

Where they needed to start is with a God who is prepared to be wounded—one who suffers alongside us, who grieves with us, who is moved by our pain, who shows up, lying on the floor alongside us, tears streaming down his face. People who pass the Dave Test know this.

They may not have an explanation for why something has happened. They may not be able to say that everything will turn out well in this life. They are not happy-clappy folk who laugh and sing their way through the graveyard. But what they can do and what they do without hesitation is say with confidence, "God is with you, God grieves alongside you, and God feels your pain."

Finding a way to say that is, I believe, the only healing vision of God worth sharing when life is hard. Things may not get better. The losses we suffer may be irretrievable. And the things that have happened to us may not have any redeeming feature. But God's presence with us—God's identification with our pain—can be a source of strength and encouragement.

That is part of the reason that I find the Christian message so compelling. That conviction is at the heart of the incarnation: God in Christ abandons the security and power that is part and parcel of being God and enters into our lives. But in the Christian message, the incarnation is not simply a message of solidarity. It is also rooted in the conviction that God's identification with our pain signals a fundamental change in human history. Death will not have the final word. Loss, pain, and sorrow are not the epitaph of human history. That message changes everything. It means that no loss is final. No sorrow or loss goes unaddressed.

That message is also present to some degree in Judaism, though not in as radical a fashion. Note, for example, the words of the Twenty-third Psalm, which declare that "the LORD is my shepherd." God does not lead the psalmist out of, but through "the valley of the shadow of death." God anoints the psalmist's head "in the presence of [his] enemies," not in their absence (KJV). There is something of that "I am with you" message in that psalm and elsewhere in the Hebrew Bible as well.[9]

But whatever your religious tradition, finding that truth is essential to hope—for us and for those we love. Embraced by the God who enters into our suffering, we discover—even in the most difficult times—that we are not alone and need not despair. The war is not over, and loss may continue to be a part of our lives, but the turning point has been reached. And God is with us, in it, all the way.

# QUESTION THREE:
## CAN I AVOID USING
## STAINED-GLASS LANGUAGE?

# QUESTION THREE:
## CAN I AVOID USING STAINED-GLASS LANGUAGE?

DAVE AND I SPEND AS MUCH TIME WITH EACH OTHER as we can. There will never be enough time. There never is.

One place where we have gone together is Colorado. When we were children, the only "real" vacation that we ever had was one in the Rocky Mountains. I don't know whether it was the drama of experiencing "real" mountains for the first time or the unique place that the trip had in our childhood, but we have both had a case of Rocky Mountain fever ever since. One of those trips was to Purgatory—Purgatory, Colorado, that is. Dave was well beyond his first surgery. He had completed a round of radiotherapy treatments, and he was on a regular oral dose of chemotherapy.

One evening I put down the beer that I was drinking and said, "Look, can I ask you something?"

"Sure," Dave responded.

"OK," I said. "Let me preface this: I'm not taking attendance, and the answer is whatever the answer is. But are you still going to church?"

Dave flinched, but only slightly.

"No, I'm not."

"Do you mind telling me why?" I asked.

"No, not at all. Two reasons really. One, there's all the stained-glass language. The churches I've attended don't speak to my life. I've listened to clergy talk over and around life's challenges without ever saying anything real about them. Either they string together a series of twenty-five-dollar words that they learned in seminary or they softball life's hard realities. I've gone to church all my life and understand what a lot of those words mean, but one way or another there is little or nothing that I can connect with.

"Two, on the rare occasion when the church does speak to me about the challenges I face, the preacher usually blows sunshine up my ass and tells me that everything will be all right. It's hard," he said, "when you've been told that you have a brain tumor to hear people tell you that God has a plan, that the best is yet to come, or that you are living a blessing in disguise."

"Saying that to someone who has a tumor that quickly claims the lives of all but 3 percent who have it is worse than useless. It's horseshit—not just false hope—to argue that at age fifty I can do more good without my surgical skills than I did with them."

The stained-glass language has troubled Dave. You and I have all heard it, and some of us have used it—that is, churchy theological language that we often fail to unpack: "God is sovereign"; "Your suffering is anticipated in the incarnation." Stained-glass language is trapped in an unreal world of ideas without a concrete point of contact with flesh-and-blood struggles.

Of course, churches aren't the only places where it is used. But the church certainly invented it, and Christians hide behind it far too often. Coming from a professionally trained stained-glass-language expert, that may sound a bit surprising. But the problems with it and the way that we use it are not all that big of a mystery.

**Problem one: Stained-glass language is not fit for helping people when life is hard.**

Stained-glass language is one kind of technical shorthand.

We all use some version of it. Engineers can hardly avoid it. Physicians rely upon it. So do academics. But plumbers, police officers, and real estate agents use it as well.

Like all technical vocabulary, "stained-glass language" is designed to name or label something that would otherwise require a sentence or a paragraph to explain. Referring to a "theology 'thingy'" just doesn't communicate. For that reason, it is great for a classroom or a lecture hall. It is also nearly useless in a hospital, emergency room, police station, or cemetery.

For example, the losses that people experience in the wake of accidents and illness and abuse and unemployment cannot be addressed by talking people about "theodicy" and "incarnation." You can unpack those words and translate them into everyday categories, but you can't use them (or at least you shouldn't).

People don't care about "the vindication of divine goodness and providence in view of the existence of evil"—that is, "theodicy."[10] They want to know, "Why did my father rape me when I was young and defenseless? If God is in control and actually gives a damn, how did this happen?"

"The embodiment of God the Son in human flesh"—that is, the "incarnation"—is a topic fit for a seminary classroom. But what people want to know is this:

"Is God in it with us—all the way—bleeding and crying, just like us?"

"Did God take my child's life in order to teach me something, or is God as devastated as I am?"

"And when, where, and how—if ever—does God plan to 'fix it'?"

That's "incarnation" worth talking about. But the word itself isn't all that useful. I'll come back to this example at the end of the chapter to illustrate what we can do.

**Problem two: Far too much of the stained-glass language that we use misrepresents the Christian message or mixes**

**in ideas from our culture that have nothing to do with the message.**

For example: *Some of us turn biblical stories into fix-it formulas.* I have lost count of the number of people I've known who were told to "name and claim it."

"Take these steps, and apply this formula."

"You and your spouse are struggling with fertility issues and have suffered through miscarriage after miscarriage? Then you are simply failing to pray with faith."

"You don't have the job or the income that was once yours? Then you must have sinned."

Frankly, there isn't a single story in the Hebrew and Christian Bible that ought to be read that way. And when they are read in that fashion, it is always because someone has forced one's own assumptions onto the text.

Modern Americans are great ones for using "steps": "three steps to the life of your dreams"; "five steps to financial security"; "ten steps to a better sex life." We all want the steps to a successful life. Ancient Jews? Not so much.

The stories of the Bible almost always have to do with God. They almost always have to do with how we can get with God's program. And they are almost always so open-ended that they suggest, but never dictate, how we ought to act. Some don't know the stories all that well. As a result, the stained-glass language can be very misleading.

For every person who offers up an easy formula for letting God solve your every problem, there is a progressive skeptic who is so obsessed with the inaccuracies and defects of the Scriptures that he or she has never bothered to plumb the wisdom of them.

To make matters worse, many of those skeptics are un-recovered "recovering fundamentalists." Those folk are too busy writing books at Easter and Christmas, telling people why they really have no reason for celebrating Easter and Christmas, to be spending time with the wisdom of those stories. So, they are really no help at all.

For example, some people get so wrapped up in debates about the origins of sin and evil (a real-life problem) and the question of whether Adam and Eve really existed (not a real-life problem) that they miss the real point of the story in Genesis 3. What the third chapter of Genesis really says, is, "Hey, this is the way it's always been. People mistake themselves for God. Then people run from God and blame one another—or snakes. Life is hard. The ground is dry. Relationships are tough. Babies cause pain. Brothers kill each other."

As a starting point, that's a good deal closer to the truth that Genesis describes and much more helpful to those who struggle.

*Still others read the biblical stories from the wrong end.*

God wins in the end, but life can still be hard. The Bible itself is filled with stories of people who struggle, suffer, doubt, and die.

But some people insist that we always read it from the "God wins" end of the story. These are the people who believe the message of the Bible, but they have also had a long, deep drink of the cultural Kool-Aid.

They've almost never suffered very long, and their motto usually is "accentuate the positive," which—as it happens—is not a Bible verse (the gospel according to Zig Ziglar, chapter 3, verse 16), but a song by Johnny Mercer.[11]

Everything is viewed through the wrong end of the binoculars. Take the life and death of Jesus for example. The logic of this dress-for-success gospel is:

- Jesus was tempted, but he couldn't give in.
- Jesus sweated blood in Gethsemane, but he really knew what was coming.
- Jesus died, but he knew he was getting back up on Sunday morning.

The problem with this approach is that Jesus becomes the God-man who has seen the movie but has never lived the sometimes-ugly reality that is life.

The essence of temptation is the ability to give in. Fear grabs us by the throat when we can't control the outcome. And the finality of death is only real to someone who is convinced that death really is the end. A Jesus who doesn't know any of that can't possibly be helpful.

I know that being told about a Savior who has only seen the movie hasn't helped Dave.

**Problem three: Stained-glass language fails to speak to our hearts and lives.**

I have worked with people who are unemployed, and, inevitably, they are all told by one well-meaning soul or another that they are "too gifted for God not to find a place for them."

Let me note a few things about this bit of stained-glass language:

When we say this kind of thing to people who are suffering the humiliation of unemployment, we dismiss their feelings. We run roughshod over the realities of the world in which they live. We offer spiritualizing advice about real-world problems that are spiritual to begin with. And we make promises that God (in all likelihood) is not going to keep.

There are millions of people who are unemployed. A large proportion of those people will stay unemployed and slip into the ranks of the sidelined and retired. Do we really believe that they are all talentless slugs and are beyond the love of God? Probably not, and, if not, whatever God might be doing, guaranteeing employment does not seem to be God's long suit.

So, if we hope to be spiritually present to those we love when they suffer, saying this kind of thing is not going to be a great help. It would be better to admit that we don't have all of the questions answered and that we are not all that confident about the future than it is to offer people a devotional word or two.

This is not, I hasten to note, permission to be the emissary of doubt and fear. But it is meant to suggest that there is a way to enter actively and in a realistic fashion into the struggles that people are facing.

Cliff, Dave's friend who is a cardiac anesthesiologist, is a great example of the balance that can be struck between honest, realistic engagement and a supportive approach that avoids fear-mongering. On the one hand, Cliff is committed to clear-eyed, down-to-earth language about his faith. "I love and let myself be loved. I tell the truth (and it's a good thing because it was getting hard to keep track of the lies). And I give my reasons for the hope that strengthens me," Cliff says.

On the other hand, he also knows enough about Dave's medical condition that he could be an ever-present voice of doom. But after every clear-eyed assessment of a difficult choice, Cliff will look for the hope that can be had in the situation. He is never unrealistic. Dave has faced tough choices thus far and there are tougher ones that lie ahead and Cliff knows that. But the hope he holds out for Dave is always real and about the spiritual choices in the moment.

At one point several months ago, for example, Dave was facing a surgery that would cut his visual field in half—a phenomenon called *hemianopia*. Cliff reviewed what Dave's doctors had to tell him about his surgery. He didn't softball the dangers, the consequences of the surgery, or the challenges of living with the results. But when the conversation was over he told his friend, "Dave, this is your choice, and you need to be comfortable with the decision. Whatever you decide, I love you, and I'm here for you."

**To abandon stained-glass language is not a matter of walking away from our faith or its vocabulary. This is about recovering the grounded genius of our faith.**

Contrary to popular prejudice, theological language arises out of real life. It is only over time that it becomes abstract and uprooted from lived situations.

If we didn't have religious language, spiritual people would be forced to invent it. In fact, they do every single day. The moment you begin to ask yourself:

"How do I explain this experience to someone else?"
"Why did this happen to me and not to others?"
"How do I help someone else find hope when times
    are difficult?"

you are using theological language.

**The key in keeping it helpful lies in making five conscious choices:**

*One, stay close to flesh-and-blood realities.* Keep your language about God and the world real. Don't ignore scientific fact, statistical realities, and human experience. People who are spiritually grounded and faithful don't depend upon fantasy. They believe that in addition to what we can hear, see, feel, touch, and smell is another dimension of reality that is at one with the world we can touch with our senses. They also believe that spiritual dimension of reality helps us make sense of that sensate world.

*Two, as much as possible, educate yourself about what you believe.* G. K. Chesterton said, "The Christian ideal has not been tried and found wanting. It has been found difficult; and left untried."[12] He was right. But at least part of the reason that those around us find "the Christian ideal" lacking is because we know far too little about it and do a lousy job of communicating it. Spiritual communities are important in this regard. No one of us has a lock on all of the truth, so spiritual truths are best understood in conversation with others.

*Three, translate whenever possible.* Technical language has its virtues, but it is almost always better to start with the lived challenges that gave rise to the language in the first place. Christianity is thread through with language that we use as shorthand. We repeat a lot of it every Sunday morning. But if we don't fully understand the words, or if the people we try to comfort don't understand them, they really aren't much good. It is better to use simple words and stories where possible. That's why Jesus told more stories than anything else.

*Four, always listen compassionately to the needs of others first.* The reason Dave and people like him have disappeared from our churches is not because they didn't want help or couldn't have benefited from it. The problem is that far too often we don't listen carefully to the ragged, nasty edges of their stories. Instead we rush in and try to correct what they are thinking, playing "spiritual whack-a-mole"—"You can't say that!" "You shouldn't think that!" "It's unfaithful to feel that way." Rather than scold those who struggle, we should give them our full attention. It is only in listening that we can be of genuine help, and there is a very good chance that we will learn more ourselves, if we are willing to listen.

*Five, avoid projecting your needs on the lives of those who suffer.* Far too often what we tell others about God and suffering is what we need or want to hear. Or, put another way, a fair amount of what passes for stained-glass language isn't Christian language at all. It's the stray pieces of broken, old glass from our own lives.

Years ago, when I was still a college student, I was involved in a "listening competition." The test we were given consisted of three rounds. In the first round, we listened to a recording of a short story read at regular speed. Then we were given an examination on the content of the story. In the second round, we listened to a second short story, but the recording was compressed and the story was told at twice the normal speed. Another examination followed. In the third and final round, we listened to two new stories told at a normal reading rate, but both stories were read at the same time. We were instructed to listen to one of the stories, but we were actually tested on both of them to test both our ability to concentrate and our residual memory of the other story.

Listening to one another when life is hard is a lot like that competition. There are always at least three parties to the conversation: our heart, the heart of the one who is struggling, and God. Whenever we let our hearts, our needs, or the stray pieces of glass from our own lives get in the way, we run the risk of frustrating God's efforts to use us and to help others.

**So, what might it look like to comfort someone without using stained-glass language? Let's go back to the idea of incarnation.**

As I said above, incarnation is the belief that Jesus (who is God) also took on human flesh. To talk about the history of that belief, the biblical evidence for it, and its place in the earliest creeds has its place. But, as I said, none of it is likely to be very helpful to someone who has lost a loved one or is struggling with loss.

But it matters and matters deeply that Jesus took on human flesh. There are at least three straightforward words of comfort that arise out of that basic truth that are worth sharing with those who suffer:

*One, Jesus is in it with us, all the way.* Jesus knows what it is to be thirsty, hungry, and in pain. He knows disappointment, frustration, anger, and grief. He has cried, struggled, and sweated blood. He is not "up there" or "out there," issuing orders or arranging car accidents and cancer. He has waded into the chaos that is our lives.

*Two, Jesus is the first to grieve.* Jesus is moved by our pain, our grief, our anger, and our sorrow. If you wonder for a moment where he is when you grieve, just pause long enough to imagine his arms wrapped around you.

*Three, we may suffer, struggle, bleed, and die, but we will not be lost or extinguished.* Jesus invades our fragile human experience, dies, and walks out of the tomb in order to say one thing:

43

"I am God. Women and men are the one thing in my creation that look like me. They are the evidence of my existence and the strength of my claim to be God. They are my beloved children, and I will not let them be destroyed. Death does not have the last word. I do."

All three statements are about spiritual realities. All three are congruent with the Christian message and Christian theology. All three are honest about just how hard life can be. But there is not a single word of stained glass in any of the three statements. And every one of them is something we can and should say to one another when life is hard.

There are times when words aren't needed at all to draw on this spiritual wisdom. One of my directees was a pastor who had a reputation for fixing problem congregations. Her bishop sent her to one troubled congregation after another. But her latest assignment was getting to her, and she was afraid that she was on the verge of a nervous breakdown. A small but really vocal group of people were on the warpath, and nothing she did seemed to blunt their criticism.

As we began to work together, I discovered that in addition to her work as a pastor, she was also a physician. In fact, she had barely finished medical school when she enrolled in seminary.

"There's a whole lot of healing going on here," I pointed out. "How long have you felt burdened to heal the world?"

A bit startled, she reflected for a few moments and then answered, "Well, probably since I was born."

"What was happening when you were born that left you feeling that way?"

"I was born on the second anniversary of my older brother's death, and my mother was in a psychotic break."

"So, you came into a world you felt obliged to resolve."

"Yeah. I suppose so."

What I recommended she do in the month that followed our meeting was go back to those early moments and ask Jesus to tell her what he would have told that little baby.

Out of that silence, she heard Jesus say, "My dear child. This was not your burden to carry. It was mine. I grieved your brother's death and held him. I stood by your brokenhearted mother. And only I can restore their lives to them."

Regardless of how much language we use to comfort those who suffer, what we do say should help people find God at the tattered edges of life, hear what God has to say, and know that God is with them.

# QUESTION FOUR:
## CAN I ADMIT THAT SOME THINGS WILL NEVER GET BETTER?

# QUESTION FOUR:
## CAN I ADMIT THAT SOME THINGS WILL NEVER GET BETTER?

THE HARDEST TRUTH TO ACCEPT IN LIFE IS THAT WE are mortal.

There is no way out of life except through the cemetery. Everyone we meet from morning to night will one day be gone and forgotten. That fact alone should remind us that some things will never get better on this side of the grave.

Some jobs go away, never to return. Some diagnoses are final (Dave often talks about having a "use by" stamp on his forehead). Divorce forecloses on certain hopes and expectations, whatever the real potential of a relationship might have been. Innocence lost is lost forever at the hands of a sexual predator. The list goes on.

The way that we react to our mortality in both its big, life-ending form and its smaller forms along life's way determines how available we can be to one another when life is hard. We can't choose *not* to be mortal. But we can choose how to react to our mortality. Sadly, a lot of us choose to isolate ourselves and leave others to struggle alone.

**The strategies we use to deal with our mortality vary.**

*The vast majority of us opt for denial.* To paraphrase Woody Allen, "We aren't afraid of dying, we just don't want to be there when it happens." You see the signs of denial throughout our culture. When someone dies, we celebrate life now, cautioning people at funerals to avoid grief. We hold memorial services instead of funerals, so that we don't need to deal with the reminders of death such as caskets and urns.

Even the famed palliative care system that we have put in place for helping patients die with dignity isn't so much about helping us face death, as it is about anesthetizing us to its approach. On more than one occasion I've seen a nurse walk into a room, inject a substance into an IV drip line, and watch the bottom fall out of a patient's respiration rate. Sometimes the conversations we all need to have about death never happen. They just get short-circuited.

*Others tie our mortality to causes that we can control, hoping to make death and other misfortunes a "rational" choice—something that happens only if you fail to eat or live well.* I've known people like this, too. Mortality and its variations on the theme are treated as the by-product of moral failure or a lack of exercise;

the underlying assumption is that "bad things really do happen (only) to bad people."

Some of the people who try to take control for all the "bad" things in life are anorexic, counting every calorie, measuring every fat gram. If someone has coronary disease or a weight problem—never mind genetics and the luck of the draw—he or she is probably just sadly lacking in discipline. It doesn't matter that Julia Child lived to be ninety-two, sloshing wine over everything and enjoining people to use cream "if you are afraid of butter," or that Winston Churchill died at age ninety-one while on a steady diet of scotch and cigars.

For these people there has to be a "reason"—a sort of failure that brings on bad things and death. Our fear of mortality is a powerful force, and under its influence are any number of empirical facts that can be ignored, even if the cemetery is filled with people who were as mortal as we are.

Others who try to make suffering a rational choice play the legalist's card. Like the person who wants to make mortality a rational choice, the legalist is even more deeply convinced that bad people get their just desserts, sooner, preferably, rather than later. One person who was an excellent and fairly public example of legalism was Jerry Falwell. Falwell was convinced that the 9/11 attacks were the result of American immorality, and he made his feelings known publicly and widely. When a firestorm of public opinion ensued, he then apologized for his statement, which he described as too subtle a theological observation to make in public.

How he thought this constituted an apology and why he thought the original statement was the least bit subtle has always escaped me. What was truly stunning, however, was the way in which he dismissed the deaths of thousands of people:

- There was no effort to defend his view of the sins mentioned.
- There was no effort to account for why this group of people died.
- There was no effort to link the behavior of the people who died (many of whom were presumably innocent of the sins Falwell had in mind) with the punishment meted out.
- There was no effort to explain the short list of sins he thought were punishable by terrorism.
- There was no effort to explain why a loving God would use evil to punish evil.

That's a fairly amazing list of omissions. But our desire to control death makes that brand of legalism perfectly intelligible to some.

*Another approach is to convince ourselves that it is life's smaller mortalities that we really fear.* There is an endless variety of heartbreak to be had along the way in life—a multitude of losses that are smaller than those brought on by death: loneliness, loss, abuse, catastrophe, and joblessness, for example. If we can't pull off denying death, then a lot of us focus—often unconsciously—on one or more of those smaller mortalities in order to distract ourselves from the harder truth.

It is easy to say that you don't dread death until it forces itself on you. And there is a certain kind of energy to be found in fighting its smaller surrogates. You can get angry with an employer for firing you. You can rail against the inability of a physician to cure you, or you can accuse her of malpractice. You can sue someone who is unfaithful to you.

I knew a man who spent a lifetime doing that. He went to war with his neighbors. He manipulated family members into awkward cul-de-sacs in which there was nothing right that they could say. He joined a church and got involved in a battle over the property, siding with his minister. Then, when it was all over, he went to war with the same minister over salaries in what was left of the church.

He pitted one of his children against two others in endless triangular games. He made first one child and then another executor of his estate until he ran out of children.

He became angry at his minister's lack of pastoral skill as a substitute for grieving his wife's death. And when he died, he used his will to disenfranchise and favor some of his children and grandchildren over the others.

He lived to be fairly old. He enjoyed relatively good health until late in life. He sucked his anger dry and hid his fear behind aggression. But, in fact, he used his anger over every loss and grievance as a means of distracting himself from the hardest kind of mortality to accept. In the end, death still came, and he was not ready.

**Whatever our approach to running from mortality, our choice to run from it has consequences.**

Some years ago I was giving a series of presentations to a class of adult learners on the subject of suffering. Over six weeks, we talked candidly about the topic and our experiences. At the end of the class a group of men and women in their late sixties and early seventies came up to me.

"Thank you for giving us the opportunity to discuss this subject in a candid, honest fashion," they said. "Honestly, we haven't been able to do this, and most of us are struggling with our own mortality in new ways. Our parents are gone, and many of our best friends and closest relatives have died. But we haven't felt free to discuss that struggle with younger members of our congregation. There is no place for a conversation of that kind, and, frankly, we are afraid that if we tell younger members of the congregation that we are struggling, we will undermine their faith and lose their respect and love."

Their admission was honest and painful. Their experience is also widespread and common.

Watching families during funerals, visiting with patients in the hospital, providing spiritual direction and counseling for the handicapped, divorced, and unemployed has convinced me that our culture is deeply shaped by an anxious flight from its own mortality. In a giant, frantic race, we have cut one another adrift, allowing those whom we love the most to experience death and loss alone.

So, when someone whom we love dies or when life hits the wall, we are often left to our own devices as well. We take a drug or a good stiff drink, bandage our wounds, grab a crutch, and hobble along behind, hoping one day to catch up and begin running again.

If we take the time to reflect on our losses at all, we can assemble the bits and pieces of wisdom that we have absorbed from random conversations, television, and pop culture, or we can reach out on Facebook. If we begin to lose pace, we can pay for professional assistance—thank God—*if* the resources are available to us.

But, heaven help you if you run out of the energy to keep up with the headlong rush into the future and, ironically, with the very thing we are trying to avoid. Our attention to your needs will be as brief as appearances will allow, and believe me, appearances count for almost nothing anymore. There are exceptions, of course, and, more to the point, exceptional people. But they are few and far between.

If our inability to admit that some things will never get better were purely a matter of personal choice, perhaps it wouldn't make so much difference. But the insistence that we aren't mortal is also a deeply spiritual choice with consequences for all of us.

Denial keeps us from being available to one another. It kills the possibility of candid, life-giving conversations about our own mortality. We run from the opportunity to learn from and support one another in times of loss, failure, abuse, and violence. If someone struggles and our first instinct is to oversimplify the problem or promise that "everything will all be all right," we inevitably alienate those who know that their circumstances in this life are beyond remedy.

When we try to hide from our mortality, we rob ourselves of intergenerational conversations and therefore of the spiritual and experiential wisdom that we might share across generations. As a result, we leave each individual to confront loss, pain, and grief as if it had never happened to anyone else, and we leave those who are older to explore the final challenge largely in pain and isolation.

Worst of all we deprive ourselves of the faith and wisdom that comes from companioning others through life's hardest challenges.

**How do we learn to admit that some things will never get better? Like so many spiritual choices, the answer is less about a formula and more about a way of being. But being and doing are a hand-in-hand deal, and doing can change us. So, there *are* some things we can do.** Try this, for example:

*First, lean into your mortality. Sit down in the cemetery and rest your head against your tombstone.* You don't need to "befriend" death or shrug it off as "a part of life." You don't need be morbid or stoic like that fun-loving couple in the painting *American Gothic*—no smiles, all grim determination, and a pitchfork. The more we are in touch with the spiritual life, the more likely it is that we will see death as a contradiction.[13] But until we own our own death as a part of the journey that lies ahead of us, we will always run from our suffering and will never be able to walk with others in theirs. So, just sit there for a while. Wrap your arms around the stone. Feel its edges and texture. Feel the earth beneath you.

*Second, trace the outline of your name.* Visualize the shape of the letters. How does your name appear there? Do you spell the whole of it out? Do you use a nickname or the name that appeared on your birth certificate? What shape is the font? How large are the letters?

*Third, trace the outline of the numbers and letters that record the date that you died.* Ooops. That last bit is something none of us can do, is it? We don't have that level of control. We have no way of knowing whether our deaths will interrupt us at the beginning of something new or in the middle of something miserable or good or when we are young or old or when we are asleep or wide awake. We can't control the world around us. Little-*m mortality* comes and goes. We win. We lose. We laugh, and we cry. Then big-*m Mortality* comes along and trumps everything else. It wipes away fortunes, buries achievements, and erases names.

*Fourth, look back, or better yet, just think about the friends, family, and choices that are a part of this day.* Think about the people closest to you. If today, were the day of big-*m* Mortality in your life, what would people say? What would you hope they would say?

Would you want them to read your resume? Review your to-do list? Rehearse your job titles? List the names of sex partners you've had? Itemize the contents of your house? Read your last tax return, making special note of what you owned

and earned? Would you want them to regale the congregation with vivid accounts of your trips to Walmart and Home
Depot?

I doubt it. But we often live life as if those things matter so
much that they ought to be mentioned at our funerals. And in
living like that, we ignore, run by, and hide from friends and
family who need our help in hard times.

**So, let's say you've worked through this spiritual exercise
and now you are finally alive to your own mortality. What are
the gifts in an exercise of that kind, and what kind of person
are you likely to become on the other side of it?**

*For one thing, you get the gift of clarity.* One of the biggest
struggles in life is getting honest with ourselves about the
nature of life. We keep trying to cut and paste life together in a
way that will make it fit the stories we tell ourselves, running
from people and situations that contradict the inner narrative
we wish were true or that we were told is true.

I am not saying that the real story is "Life's a b——, and
then you die." Life is filled with far too many good things and
beauty for that kind of nihilism. But what I am saying is that
life is too fragile, too short, and too precious to be spent in
ways that don't merit repeating at your graveside. When you
do the kind of exercise I describe above, you suddenly realize
that every moment of our lives is simply a series of moments
in which we can choose to love and care for one another, and
those are, in fact, the only life-defining choices we control.

*Second, by getting real about your mortality, you get the gift of
maturity.* I went to a class years ago on parenting adolescents.

The teacher, who was a psychologist, argued that the problem with teenagers is that they believe in "the three *I*'s"—"they think that they are immortal, invincible, and infertile." He was right. But the problem with a lot of us as adults is that we continue to believe in the first two "*I*'s" long after it is clear we are neither immortal nor invincible.

The difficulty, of course, is that there is nothing about immaturity that gets us closer to owning the fullness of life, and adolescents are usually incapable of walking with those who suffer. By contrast, those who have grasped the fact of their mortality are better prepared to live life as they find it. They are also the ones who are better able to care for others because they are people who do not live in constant dependence upon others to make their lives possible.

*None of this means that life needs to be lived in grim resolve. Those who are aware of their mortality are also given the gift of life lived with abandonment, freedom, and urgency.*

Jesus is a wonderful example in this case. He is the paragon of maturity. He is fully aware of his mortality. In fact, Luke's observation that Jesus "determined to go to Jerusalem" suggests that his brief adult life was lived out of a serious sense of mission, and he knew that his arrival in Jerusalem would precipitate a crisis in his ministry that would risk his life (Luke 9:51).

But he isn't morose. He goes fishing. He probably did some carpentry. He parties. He hangs out with people who are struggling, unloved, lost, and sick. He laughs and eats. He even knows how to make a good bottle of wine.

By contrast, running from our mortality is a burden. We live in fear. We calculate every move and second-guess every choice. Jesus was surrounded by people like that, and part of what is thread through the Gospel stories is the freedom with which he lived in the middle of all that fearful deliberation. He was never dominated by it.

We can live with that kind of freedom, too. We can claim the unexpected freedom that lies on the other side of owning our own mortality. We can let go of the lies that we tell ourselves and one another. We can sit without flinching with those for whom life is not going to get better. We can be available to love, laugh, and hug even if there is nothing to be said or done.

Our friend Harry was one of those guys. He hit the bottle hard and hit the bottom harder—twice. But instead of letting the experience drive him deeper into addiction, and instead of becoming completely absorbed with the task of caring for himself, he went to work in a shelter for alcoholics, drug addicts, and the homeless. He went back to school and got a variety of certifications and degrees to help him in his work. And he spent a lifetime trying to help other men and women climb out of the pit. Harry lived with joy. He was a great big bear of a man who knew how to laugh, how to have a great time, and how to hug, encourage, and challenge those around him. And he did all of those things until his dying day.

You don't need to go to work in a shelter for the homeless to be the kind of person who passes the Dave Test. But if you want to be available to those you love when life is is at its shattered ends, the best way to get there may be to ask God to help you learn how to hug your tombstone. Like Harry, those are the ones who can admit that sometimes things are not going to get better but are not controlled by it. They live above it and through it, in love with others.

# QUESTION FIVE:
## CAN I GIVE UP TRADING IN MAGIC AND SUPERSTITION?

# QUESTION FIVE:
# CAN I GIVE UP TRADING IN MAGIC AND SUPERSTITION?

SEVERAL DAYS BEFORE CHRISTMAS IN 2003, QUINTIANA, the daughter of authors Joan Didion and John Dunne, fell ill and was hospitalized with what was first diagnosed as flu, then pneumonia, and finally as septic shock. She was put into an induced coma and placed on life support. Just hours before New Year's Eve, John suffered a massive heart attack and died. Four weeks later, Quintiana would recover, only to collapse some weeks later and suffer a massive head injury that would require hours of surgery and a torturous recovery. Writing about the uncharacteristic rituals that marked her behavior in those early hours after John's death and in the wake of the trauma that followed, Didion observes:

I see now that my insistence on spending that first night alone was more complicated than it seemed, a primitive instinct. Of course I knew that John was dead. Of course I had already delivered the definitive news to his brother and to my brother and to Quintana's husband. *The New York Times* knew. The *Los Angeles Times* knew. Yet I myself was in no way prepared to accept this news as final: there was a level on which I believed that what had happened was reversible. That was why I needed to be alone. . . . I needed to be alone so that he could come back. This was the beginning of my year of magical thinking.[14]

Our tendency to resort to magic is not surprising. Life confronts us with intractable realities:

- "Your husband is dead."
- "The swelling caused by the trauma has compromised your daughter's brain."
- "You have pancreatic cancer."
- "Wind shear crashed the plane."
- "There are 'x'-number of people who are unemployed."
- "One out of every 'x'-number of marriages fails."
- "The sex slave trade continues to ensnare 'x'-number of women worldwide."

Magic offers formulas and steps for bending and controlling the terrible realities around us: "Say these words, follow this ritual, and life will change." That is why some of the most rational and reasonable people I know avoid the number thirteen, throw salt over their shoulders, and fret about black cats that cross their path.

This kind of behavior would be easy enough to laugh off if magic and religion were kept at a safe distance from each other. Magical thinking in its purest form is not hard to recognize.

Sometimes, magic offers theological justifications for behavior that, in truth, has no theological justification: "You can be cured, if you just believe"; "Name it and claim it; you will get a new job." When we wait for Jesus to pull a rabbit out of a hat or we manipulate God to meet our needs, we court disillusionment with God. We add spiritual isolation to our struggles. Spiritually we stay focused in the wrong place, looking for deliverance rather than for strength, for cures instead of healing. And we do this when, in truth, our suffering and the suffering of those we love is precipitated either by factors completely beyond our control or by moral choices, not magic.

**The invitation of this question in the Dave Test is to set aside our obsession with magical thinking about the hard places in life and to walk in freedom with God, even when life is broken, focused on what we can do.**

*Step one: Pray for deliverance, and then expect to live in intimate dependence upon God.*

Nothing has rocked my world the way Dave's illness has. I have been with people who have died at an advanced age, and I have spent hours in the hospital and at the graveside with families who have lost loved ones to tragic accidents. I have entered into that space, empathetically, and I have been moved by their grief. In every case, including Dave's, I have prayed for deliverance. I don't pray those prayers because I necessarily believe that deliverance will come. Loss happens. Death comes to us all. I pray those prayers because I believe that prayer is a conversation with God, and to be honest with God is to pray well. God does not score our prayers based upon our capacity for stoic acceptance. God does not evaluate our prayers based on their theological sophistication. Prayers open us to God so that God can walk alongside us.

I long with every ounce of my strength for Dave to survive. He is my younger brother. My "big brother job" is to take care of him, and I want this for him. I also want this for me. I don't hesitate to pray for him to survive.

At the same time, I know that his diagnosis is terminal. No one with his tumor has yet survived. Physicians do not even use the word *remission* in connection with his cancer. And he has already lived longer than anyone expected.

Where do we live in moments like these? Do we abandon prayers for deliverance and succumb to the inevitable? No. Whatever the loss or struggle, it is our task as God's creation to struggle for the moments of love, grace, and creativity that is part and parcel of the God-breathed lives that we have been given. As long as we have breath, strength, and time, that is what we need to do. The warmth and depth of our relationships, the things of beauty and genius, and the nobility of human achievement would not exist if we succumbed to death and lived like fatalists. Think of the gifts that are ours as a race that exist because our predecessors lived in hope of deliverance, but often on the brink of destruction.

At the same time, as painful as it has been to admit it to myself, I know that I will lose Dave. We are a long way from a cure for his illness. He has no special claim to immunity. I have no special grounds for asking that he be the exception to the rule. Everyone he knew who had the same tumor when he received his diagnosis is dead—many of them for years now. Sisters have lost brothers, brothers have lost sisters, and parents have lost children.

There comes a point in our mortal lives when striving, creating, fighting, and struggling comes to an end. Then, in looking back, we realize that as important as those moments have been, life has only one deep purpose: to live in ever-greater dependence upon God. Not because God uses our loss to force us to that point, but because loss radicalizes life and underlines its true nature. This means setting aside our need to think magically. It means trusting that no matter how bad things are on the other side of our struggle—even on the other side of death—God will be there to care for us in ways that we cannot anticipate.

*Step two: Focus on healing, not on curing.*

We are a fix-it culture. For every illness, there is a cure; for every challenge, there is a fix. It is an enormous strength, the engine of invention and exploration. But truth be told, the end comes. On this side of that divide every cure and every fix is specific to a particular problem. Every cure is temporary. By contrast, healing is comprehensive and eternal.

That is why Jesus' approach to curing the illnesses of those he met was marked by such strange contradictions. He touched people with tenderness, made the lame walk, helped the mute speak, helped the deaf hear. But he also walked away from long lines of people waiting for help. He did not go to Jerusalem General Hospital and clear the wards. And many of the healings he did were explicitly tied to spiritual needs, not the physical.

The miracles are not the goal or end-all of Jesus' ministry; they are signs of the coming of the kingdom of God. They are the transitory and partial foreshadowers of something that will be permanent and comprehensive. To focus on cure, then, diverts us from life's true purpose, and it misunderstands the way that God works in the world. Some miseries and losses may be reversed, but God's work promises to embrace the whole of life, and in its fullness—which is yet to come—God promises that healing work will be comprehensive.

Put positively, to focus on healing in a world that offers only temporary respite from suffering means accepting life's imperfections and tattered edges. It means celebrating the good things in life that reflect God's love for and goodness to us. And—when life is hard—it means resting in the knowledge that nothing good in this life is forever lost but is kept safe for us by God. It also means resisting the temptation to use magical understandings of prayer as a means of end-running the need to rest in and depend upon God.

I have been unemployed twice. It is not easy. Losing a job challenges our sense of self-worth, control, and value. It is a hard place that upends life dreams, and any fix for it in the shape of a new job can take months or years to find. Even then the painful aspects of the experience linger, forever changing your view of the work world and relationships.

In those long interludes, my own focus on healing has been to attend as closely as possible to the spiritual work at the center of that experience, letting go of understandings of self-worth that are rooted in the views of others and of the cultural patterns that suggest that "we are what we do." I have sought to live into God's love for me and the goodness of my life as God's child. And I have tried to let God take me back through my life to free me from the things in the past that make me dependent upon the fragile and transitory aspects of the work world.

That doesn't mean I haven't looked for a job. But many of us never find alternative employment, and there was no guarantee that I would find it. Dave knows that there is no cure for his illness, so he has enrolled in clinical trials that may lead to discoveries that will save the lives of others. Whatever the alternatives open to us, in moments when we are not in control, the most important thing that we can do in an otherwise unpleasant experience is the one thing that is always possible: live in ever-deeper connection with God, and let God sit with us in the middle of that pain to listen for what we can learn that will bring us healing.

*Closely related, then, is step three: We need to wait in hope.*

If the progress that we see being made in our own lives and the world around us is fragmentary and ragged, it is not because God has decided to give up magic. Nor does is it mean that we are not praying well or that we don't believe deeply enough in the work of God. Things are fragmentary and ragged because God is not finished.

Complaining that our ragged world and our tattered lives are evidence that God is not willing to help us or that our prayers are unheard is like complaining that a play is like complaining during the intermission that a play is incomplete. Biblical stories about "the end of all things" are not about "pie-in-the-sky by-and-by." They are not about the "carrot" and the "stick" that you get for virtues or vice in the next life. They are about the healing work that God has begun but has not yet completed. The first two spiritual exercises I have suggested are not, then, an exercise in stoicism or grim resignation. They are a hopeful way of being in the world.

We tend to think of hope as a fairly abstract commodity, as simple optimism or positive thinking. But this kind of hope is rooted in the confidence that God is on our side and is actively at work in the world in ways that will reverse even the deepest of life's losses. That kind of confidence—call it faith—makes for courage and resilience. It is the stuff of those who walk alongside those who suffer, not those people who came to see magic made. If we pray for deliverance and live in intimate dependence upon God, focus on healing and not on cure, and wait in hope, we can be that kind of people to those whom we love.

# QUESTION SIX:
## CAN I STOP BLOWING SMOKE?

# QUESTION SIX:
## CAN I STOP BLOWING SMOKE?

"WHAT IN HELL AM I GOING TO DO WITH MY LIFE THAT is going to be more of a blessing to other people than what I was doing?" That's what Dave said when people told him that he had lost his eyesight and his ability to function as a surgeon because God had bigger things for him to do. Dave's conversation partners were well meaning, but ultimately they were blowing smoke. They were wrapping a bright, sunny scenario around an unmitigated disaster.

**His experience is not unique, and, truth be told, the church isn't alone in "blowing smoke." We all do it, and in doing it we lie to ourselves.**

Some years ago, I gave a series of presentations to a group of adults on the subject of suffering. In the course of the conversation, I noted that God does not orchestrate misfortune:

"God does not launch wars, induce the growth of cancer cells, arrange car accidents, cripple children, or cause infertility." That last phrase made one couple visibly angry. (What they didn't know is that the last example came from my own struggle with infertility and the desire to have children.)

Although it took a few days to discover why they were so agitated, I finally identified the problem. According to other people in the class, they had struggled with infertility. As a result they had provided a foster home for several orphaned children. They were convinced that it was God who had made them infertile for the express purpose of leading them into this "ministry of love." On that last note, I realized why they were angry. What I had said contradicted the way that they understood God and their lives. It also raised questions about the animating force behind the relationships that they had with their foster children.

I have no doubt that what they were doing was a powerful witness to the love of God. But I don't think that God *made* them infertile. What I do believe is this: they met a tragic emptiness in the lives of the children that they fostered by drawing creatively and sacrificially on the vacancy in their own lives. That's a powerful witness to the children who are the beneficiaries of their love, to those who suffer loss and wonder, "Now what?" and to those who might let similar losses embitter and harden them. But they couldn't see that, and I wasn't able to convince them.

Why couldn't they tell themselves the truth about their infertility? Why "blow smoke" or "deceive" themselves? After all, the way in which they understood their experience robbed their efforts of something heroic and faithful. And, although they were not yet aware of it, they had also "created" a God who is cruel, manipulative, and impossible to worship.

We all "blow smoke" from time to time. Why?

*Three overlapping needs are consciously—and even more often, unconsciously—at work: control, comfort, and meaning.*

**First, when life is at its frayed ends, we blow smoke because we long for control.** That's an understandable and a completely human desire. Of course, the problem is that we are not in control. So, what we want most, we can't have. But rather than confront the reality that we don't control everything and then deal with it, we blow smoke. We lie to ourselves and to one another in a hundred and one ways in order to maintain the illusion of control.

Of course, all we do is postpone confronting the truth. Sooner or later we all face the realization that we are not in control. But we do a fairly good job of fooling ourselves, relying on one of two strategies for crowding the truth in the margins of our consciousness.

*One strategy is to claim "little sovereignties" for ourselves.* There are whole consultancy practices and self-help programs built on this approach, and the message is always roughly the same:

"You are a powerful person."
"You can choose how you react."
"You can shape the realities around you."

In other words, *you* are sovereign. Your future is in your hands.

There is a certain amount of truth in this message, of course. We are all made in the image of God. We are endowed with freedom and creativity. But there is a fragile difference between being made in the image of God and thinking that we are God. We cannot control everything.

When life frays at the edges, we may be able to convince ourselves for a while that we can manage. But truth be told, we don't always have choices. The choices that we make do not necessarily alter the realities with which we live. And there are hard places where we run out of life with which to make choices. That's why more than one friend has told me that it was sitting on the floor and finally acknowledging his or her powerlessness over addiction and the suffering that goes along with it that opened the doors to recovery.

*A second strategy is to seek a sense of control by looking to "big" sovereignty, projecting the kind of control that we wish we had onto our views of God.* It may seem strange to complain about people believing that God is in control. After all, everyone who believes in God believes that God is in control in one way or another. And from the vantage point of faith, that's legitimately comforting control.

But the problem here isn't so much about thinking God is in charge. It's about the way that we think about God being in charge. When we describe cancer, abuse, war, and disaster as "the will of God," we make God a monster whom no one can or should worship.

**Second, all of us look for comfort, too:** a break or a distraction, in order to rest, escape the stress we experience, or marshal our strength. Suffering takes us to the limits of our ability to cope physically, emotionally, and spiritually. Even the bravest and strongest of us cannot live on the fraying edges of life 24/7. Some of us find that relief by laying aside our concerns, by going on vacation, or by going on retreat. Some distract themselves with a book, a movie, a hobby, or dinner with close friends. Still others find silence and prayer a source of comfort.

*But almost all of us also seek a certain amount of relief by framing the suffering that we experience in a fashion that gives us the strength to carry on.* This is where we get into trouble. It is not that it's inappropriate to look for comforting ideas. The problem is with the ideas themselves.

*One mistake that we make is confusing cultural values with religious truths.* You've heard these before. We say things to one another that arise out of our cultural values and present them as verses from the Bible. But many of them are either not in the Bible at all or are built on Bible verses in ways that the writers never intended. For example:

- "What doesn't kill you makes you stronger." The Bible? No. It is from Friedrich Nietzsche[15] and from there into the American bloodstream through singer Kelly Clarkson.[16] And if Nietzsche's own life is any example, it is pretty cold comfort.[17]

- "God doesn't give us more than we can bear." First
Corinthians 10:13? That's certainly the verse that is
often offered to shore up these comforting words. But
is that how the passage should be read? No. The Greek
for *tempted* can also be translated as *tested*. But the context has nothing to do with suffering, pain, or loss, as
the reference to the children of Israel makes clear in
verses 1-11.

So, the above verse in question should be translated as:
God "won't allow you to be tempted beyond your abilities."
Saint Paul is urging the Corinthians to remain faithful and to
remember that there is no temptation to sin that can overwhelm
and destroy their relationship with God, if they remain faithful. It says nothing about suffering. It has nothing to do with
God's gate-keeping life's misfortunes or sending us tempta-
tions to see if we will fail.

*The other mistake that we make when we look for comfort comes
from reading religious and spiritual truths exclusively through the
lens of our own lives.* We ignore the larger human experience
and, instead, generalize from our own experiences.[18]

For example: One man who survived the attack on New
York's World Trade Center on September 11, 2001, explained
his escape to a reporter, observing, "God cares for God's own."
It is important to remember that the man who was asked this
question was in shock and was suffering from "survivor's
guilt." So, it is important to cut him some slack.

However, if he had reflected on it, he might have realized that the comforting lie that he told himself could do nothing but anger and discomfort the family and friends of those who did not survive. Did he really think that the people who escaped from those buildings were the only ones who God loves? Did he think that God only saved those who were worthy? Or did he think that God lost track of a few people in all the confusion?

I doubt that he thought any of those things. But what he did do is generalize from his own experience. It may have comforted him. It was of no comfort to anyone else, nor did it make sense. Yet, we do this far too often and not just when we are in shock.

**Third, we blow smoke because we want life to make sense and to have meaning.** For some of us, this is the hardest challenge of all when life comes unraveled. We all need for life to make sense. The efforts and plans that we make are shaped by a certain logic. We expect virtue and effort to be rewarded, love to be returned, commitments to be honored, and the good to live a long time. So, we turn ourselves inside out to make life make sense.

A good friend of mine, for example, assumes that there is an upside to every event, no matter how much pain or dislocation may be involved, because—as he puts it—"we are always making progress." But how can that be true? Some people are overwhelmed by grief. Death brings an end to every kind of progress. New alliances and growth can sometimes be built on the ruins of war. But war also erases the hopes and dreams of generations.

Human history itself also resists the interpretation that we are always making progress. We have just exited the most violent century in history. The new one is not off to a wonderful start. Although there are pockets of social and technological progress, the world is hardly moving forward in lockstep. And in some cases, the "progress" we make simply surfaces new kinds of suffering.

The ancient Jews believed that Genesis 1 taught that in the beginning "chaos" prevailed and God's claim to be God was made good by conquering the chaos—over and over again. The message of Genesis is that God will conquer it, but chaos is a part of the world. If that is the case—and there is ample evidence in the world around us to suggest it is—then meaninglessness and absurdity are bound to be features of the world around us.

So how do we offer hope without blowing smoke?

**One, we should acknowledge that to say, "God is in control," does not and cannot mean that everything that happens is either good or God's will.** There's a long debate about the subject of God's sovereignty across Christian history. But, broadly speaking, there have been two views of the way that works. The best way to illustrate is to use an analogy for life's journey by comparing two kinds of ships. (Sailors, give me some slack here. This is an analogy, so I'm talking in relative terms, and I know that ships don't quite work this way.)

*Especially in hard times, we want God to exercise control by act-ing like a ship with an engine.* This is more or less the version of divine control that we would want to have if we were God: no variation in the course that's not dictated by the captain. No stops along the way that the captain didn't have in mind. We would want a straight, predictable movement from port A to port B. In other words, nothing would happen that God didn't want to happen, and nothing would happen that didn't have a purpose.

Many of us (such as the couple I mentioned earlier in the chapter) prefer this kind of divine control because we prefer to think that nothing happens to us that is finally and really unpleasant, hard, or devastating. The problem is that there is nothing about human history that suggests that this is the case. The good die young. Millions are swept away by wars and disease. We kill one another. We persecute, abuse, and tor-ment one another. The evidence that not everything is good and beautiful just goes on and on. Simply read one newspaper. The problem with this view then is that it forces us to believe that God is either (1) a monster or (2) not very good at running the universe.

*But there is a different kind of divine control that is possible. One that is more like a sailboat.* On this particular reading of divine sovereignty, the ship leaves from port A. Along the way it is blown off course. It runs aground, and it does some other things that the captain would really prefer it didn't do. Nonetheless, because the captain is endlessly adaptable and because the captain (that is, Jesus) is in the ship with us all along the way, it finally reaches port B.

On the way, the crew of "God's sailboat" learns that the most important part of the journey has less to do with what happens, less to do with where the ship goes, and a lot more to do with sticking close to the captain and learning how to be a crew.

This picture of divine control accords much better with the gospel and with human experience. It also keeps us from saying things about suffering that are hurtful and alienating to one another. The fact of the matter is, as Harold Kushner and good Jews from the beginning of time have noted, "bad things really do happen to good people" and to bad people and to average people.[19] God is in control, and eventually "God wins." But there are times when life sucks.

**Two, tell the truth in love.** Truth without love can be abusive and crushing. Love without truth can be evasive and soft. Together, they offer reliable help. A true companion in times of suffering knows this and avoids the extremes: love that hides the truth from those whom we care for and truth-telling that is done in ways that are devastating.

There are no clear "rules" for getting that balance right. Far too much of the companioning process depends upon the nature of the relationship we have with others, the nature of the moment itself, and the nature of information.

*We may or may not be empowered by the nature of our relationship to share certain information with someone we love.* There are professional rules of confidentiality to be observed. We may have a primary or secondary relationship with someone. It is worth asking ourselves:

- Is this my information to share? Should someone else be the one to share it?
- In imparting that information to someone else, am I triangulating?
- Am I motivated to share this information because the person involved has a right to that information and needs it to make an intelligent decision?
- Or, put another way, am I hiding information that will be important to make a realistic assessment about next steps?

*Timing is important as well.* We can endlessly postpone telling the truth, convincing ourselves that "now is not the right time." We can also indulge the ego-driven desire to be "the only one who will tell the truth."

It is worth asking ourselves: is the person involved in a fragile state, or will the person need support and assistance in processing this information? Are support and assistance available? Is the person in a physical, mental, and emotional state that will allow him or her to process the information? Or is there someone charged with this person's care who has clearly and legitimately assumed responsibility for making decisions? It is also worth doing a "gut check" to be sure that our motives behind telling the truth or withholding it are not emotionally self-serving or patronizing and paternalistic (or maternalistic).

*The information involved can also vary, and it is worth asking ourselves about the nature of what we say to those who suffer: is what we "know" a fact or an opinion?* Knowing that facts are often subject to interpretation, are we clear with those who suffer about the contingent nature of the truth we are telling them? Do we have firsthand or secondhand knowledge? Is the knowledge of a sufficiently technical nature (legal, medical, or financial, for example), that there are others who should be involved?

**Three, honor the image of God in those we love.** *To blow smoke distorts or hides the truth. To blow smoke is to manipulate.* It connives or coerces those we love to make the choices we think are "good for them." It patronizes, assuming that we know more and better understand the choices that should be made. Worst of all, shading or hiding the truth assumes a role that belongs to God alone. It robs those we love of choice and, therefore, of the agency that belongs to the children of God.

*Honesty empowers those we love.* It recognizes the integrity of their journey. It creates a space in which the one who struggles can find new opportunities for spiritual growth.

**Finally, remember that telling the truth involves more than delivering a message.** *Talk is cheap.* Even when we impart information that is hard to hear, it is far easier to drop the information and run.

*If the truth is really told in love, then that implies a relationship.* And a loving relationship involves walking with the person for whom we care. That can be a demanding journey. The person in our care may or may not be able to come to grips with the truth right away. It may take some time to formulate a response or make the necessary choices. And when life really unravels, sharing truth in love may simply entail walking through the ensuing pain with the one we love.

Remember that knowing the truth is often the beginning of a difficult journey, not the key to its resolution. But loving and allowing ourselves to be loved on that journey is a far better choice than hiding behind a smoke screen.

# QUESTION SEVEN:
# CAN I SAY SOMETHING THAT HELPS?

# QUESTION SEVEN:
## CAN I SAY SOMETHING THAT HELPS?

JACK, A FRIEND OF MINE WHO RUNS A CIGAR SHOP, was telling me that one of his customers showed up after a long absence. "Hey, where have you been?" Jack inquired. "My wife had a serious illness, and I've been spending all of my time caring for her. She died a month ago," the customer responded. "I have to admit," Jack confessed, "I was pissed that he even told me. I was thinking, hey, man, I'm your cigar guy. Why are you telling me this? I don't know what to say."

Let's admit it, speaking to a suffering friend can be hard and scary, and no one is going to get it right all the time. But, as this chapter will suggest, there are two steps we can take to increase the likelihood that we will say things that really help our friends. First, we can examine where our ideas come from and where they lead us (I outline a three-part process for doing just that). Second, we can begin to ask ourselves not "what should I say in this hard situation" but "what can we— my friend and I—say together?"

So, first, let me say more about the three questions we can ask ourselves before we say anything to those who suffer.

**One of the most basic questions we can ask before we say anything is, "Where did this idea originate?"** The origin of an idea may tell us something about the operative assumptions behind it and the larger system of thought into which it fits. It's not about deciding on the validity of ideas based solely upon where they came from. As one of my professors noted when I was in college, "All truth is God's truth." Nor am I suggesting that where an idea originates tells us everything about its value. Just as words have an etiology (or origin) but may come to mean something very different, so ideas can acquire new meaning.

For example, some people believe that everything that happens to us was meant to happen to us or was willed to happen to us by God or by some force beyond our control. This is an idea that has complex origins. To some degree its origins are in our desire to account for events in our lives that are out of our control and out of keeping with our hopes and desires. So, its origins are, in part, primal and emotional.

As a more formal idea, the notion of "fate" is worked out in the philosophy of the Stoics, who believed there were forces that shaped our lives. Elsewhere it appears in ancient Greek religion, which held that there were actually gods—

three sisters, in fact: Clotho, Lachesis, and Atropos—who were assigned the role of determining the fate of human beings.

In Christianity, some of the church's great teachers lend some weight to the idea as well. Augustine suggests that those who talk about fate might do so, but he argues that they should refer to God and not fate. And the great Reformation figures such as John Calvin and Martin Luther talk about "predestination."

The fact that some of the church's great teachers held these ideas does not mean that all Christians believe that God works in this way. There are as many Christians—perhaps more—who believe that although God is control of human history, God does not orchestrate the details of our lives. In other words, God did not decide whether you would have a bagel or scrambled eggs for breakfast today.

What does this tell us, and how does it help us in our efforts to encourage those who grieve and struggle? First, it offers perspective. The notion that when we suffer loss it was meant to be is clearly rooted in emotional needs to some degree. Second, whatever its place in Christian theology, the pedigree of this idea is far more complex than a reference to Christian history would imply. Third, although there are distinguished voices in Christian history that promote this understanding of our struggle with life's hard places, those voices are hardly the only voices.

You will need to make your own critical assessment of how that might help you encourage others. For my own part, it means that I don't feel obliged to argue that my dear friends lost their daughter because God willed it

**The second question we can ask is: "Do my ideas cohere or hang together?"** Here, again, this is a question with its limits. Emerson was right when he said "foolish consistency" can be "the hobgoblin of little minds,"[20] and sometimes divergent ideas can give us multiple ways of looking at a spiritual challenge that are not necessarily mutually exclusive.

But coherence has its virtues. Ideas that hang together can point you along a spiritual path that lengthens and thrives by virtue of the way in which you are brought back time and again to ways of thinking about a spiritual challenge.

Take, for example, our ideas about prayer. You could entertain notions about prayer that suggest that God can be manipulated magically. Get the words right, make sure your attitude is good, then God will respond. Or you might assume that prayer is about a conversation with the God who loves you and who is trustworthy, regardless of the prayers that might seem to go unanswered.

On the whole, however, if you lurch between prayer as magic and prayer as relationship, the experience would probably be deeply frustrating and confusing. Eventually you would probably opt for one view or the other, if not abandon prayer altogether.

I can promise that if you begin to think of prayer in terms that emphasize the relationship and God's overwhelming love, you will begin to find prayer more meaningful and fulfilling. One of the best ways to see if you are being coherent in your prayers is to listen to what you pray and ask yourself questions like these:

Does this prayer build up my relationship with God?

Am I bringing all of myself, warts and all, to this relationship?

Is this prayer an honest reflection of what I am thinking and feeling?

Do I "listen" for God to lead me, or do I do all the talking?

Does this prayer rely on the conviction that God loves me better than I can ever love myself?

Does my prayer reflect the conviction that cure might happen in this life, but complete healing is available only in the next life?

Paying attention to whether or not your spiritual ideas are coherent can be life giving. They can center your life and provide a basis for spiritual growth and deepening.

**The third question we can ask is, "Where will this idea take me?"** I have a friend who suffered terribly from cerebral palsy as a child, and it confined him to a wheelchair. He has spent all of his life there, and at the age of twenty-eight, he has already had both hips replaced to deal with the effects of long-time confinement to the chair.

A member of his church came up to Justin not long ago and declared, "Justin, I am praying for you, and God is going to get you out of this chair." Fortunately, Justin had the maturity to thank him for the care implicit in his statement but then rightly told the man, "If getting me out of this chair is all that God has in store for me, then I'm ready to die now." Justin wanted much more from God than simply to walk.

The most important issue for Justin's friend at church is that a cure is found for Justin's illness and that Justin get out of his wheelchair. Justin could focus there. He could wait for a cure. He could even postpone living his life until he is cured. After all, who wouldn't want to walk and, if the purpose of prayer is to "get a cure" from God, why not focus there?

Justin, however, had the maturity to say, "That's not where I can live, and it's not where I should live. I have an irreversible condition. That's a fact of my life, but my condition and my life are two different things. God has other things in mind for my life, things that matter more than getting out of this chair. Whatever my physical state might be, God loves me, wants a relationship with me, and believes I am worthy and valuable." In other words, Justin's own approach to prayer takes him in a very different direction. His friend's prayers would inevitably lead to a futile quest for a cure. Justin's approach allows him to live and celebrate the life that he has.

It's important to ask where an idea will take us. Does it lead us to a dead end? Does it prompt us to pray for the wrong things? Does it distract us from life-giving and constructive living?

**Can we ask these critical questions on the spur of the moment? To some degree, yes, but it is far better now to begin giving thought to the way in which we understand our own struggles and the struggles of others.** What we share with one another will be more carefully considered. It can be tested against the wisdom of millennia-long traditions. We can test our understanding of suffering in a more dispassionate setting. And the answers can become more a part of who we are.

The last of those changes is a goal that cannot be accomplished overnight. It requires a different way of evaluating life on its frayed edges. It requires new ways of seeing that become a part of who we are. Ultimately that is the critical difference between applying information and growing in wisdom. The application of information is a temporary fix. Growth in wisdom is a journey of transformation.

**Inevitably, of course, the question that arises is: apart from the well-being of those I love, what standard do I use to determine what I might say?** That is a question that readers will need to answer for themselves. And the answers that each of us will give will likely differ to one degree or another from those closest to us.

Dave is a Baptist. I am an Episcopalian. We both grew up as Methodists. He went to medical school. I went to seminary. Those differences alone mean that we see the world somewhat differently.

Being honest about those differences and talking about them openly has been important for both of us. We've had long talks about difficult subjects:

- How radical should we be in the treatment of an illness like his?

- What is the best way to spend the days left?
- What do we tell our children?
- What are the messages we leave behind?
- When will it be time to stop fighting?
- How will he know? If he can't make that decision, how will I know?
- What awaits us beyond the grave?

We are both aware that we can't answer those questions for ourselves or discuss them with each other purely on the basis of what makes us "feel" better or purely on subjective judgments about our well-being. The truth needs to factor in as an important element in answering any question with integrity, and the stakes are even higher when life is hard.

Dave would put it differently, I am sure. But for me, that standard of truth is shaped by a distinctively Christian view of life, the sources for which are the Scriptures and tradition of the church. Those resources do not dictate what I say to Dave or to anyone who is struggling. The path from Scripture and tradition to the issues in our own modern lives is not that simple, given the differences between the setting in which we live and the setting in which those resources were shaped and written.

When life sucks, the search for a faithful response cannot be reduced to such formulas as "The Bible says it, and that settles it" or "What would Jesus do?" But that's not really a problem. We are not called to simply parrot biblical passages. We are not Jesus and—apart from some perennial similarities such as human emotions and basic physical needs—our world is very different from the world that was at any point in the past.

By thinking and living in ways that are faithful to the truths at the heart of the Bible and the church's great teachers, it is possible to craft a response to life's hard places that draws deeply on the Christian faith, that hangs together, and that takes us to a place that is faithful to God's purpose for our lives.

Dave and I have talked a lot about that effort. He points out that the discovery he has made in the middle of his illness is that there is a place that still remains in which he can connect more deeply with God, his family, his friends, and himself. It's not a space that God created by giving him cancer. It is not the thing that God wanted to teach him through his illness. It is something that he has learned in the middle of an illness, the causes of which are random and uncontrolled, by giving himself again and again to God in the middle of a situation God grieves as much as Dave grieves.

As hard as it has been, the struggle to get there has been a gift not just to Dave but to me as well. The question is not really, "What can I say?" The question is, "What can *we* say about *our* lives, which differ from each other, but which are all marked by suffering sooner or later?" When we are willing to ask that question, there is a place where God nurtures the wisdom, courage, and grace that we all need. We learn that we need not fear our mortality, that the way in which we give ourselves in love to God and to one another matters more than what happens to us, and that healing awaits us—if not in this life, then in the next.

# QUESTION EIGHT:
## CAN I GRIEVE WITH OTHERS?

# QUESTION EIGHT:
## CAN I GRIEVE WITH OTHERS?

ON THE DAY THAT DAVE CALLED TO LET ME KNOW that he had a terminal disease, my life changed. The change was dramatic and unwelcome. The diagnosis was itself an occasion for grief. Although Dave has done well so far, that grief has never really lifted, but it doesn't color everything.

We laugh. We trade trivial stories. We kvetch about politics and the rising price of gasoline. When we miss connecting, the opening line of his voice mail message is almost always, "Hey, Fred, hope you're having a good evening..." We exchange stories about our children. We ask about each other's wife. I commiserate with him about the Tennessee Titans. He almost sympathizes with me over the performance of the Dallas Cowboys.

We've spent time together. It isn't all grief and morbidness over the guy who has the "use by" date stamped on his forehead. We tried racquetball. He gave me a hard time about beating a guy who is half-blind. We went deep-sea fishing. The surgery has made him violently susceptible to seasickness. So we weren't out as long as we expected to be. We've spent long hours in his cabin in the Rocky Mountains, where he pointed out that I had no reason to take pride in beating a guy who has a brain tumor at Scrabble. In spite of his illness, he walked me into the ground trekking mountainsides in snowshoes.

We have also talked to each other every day, morning and night, for over seven years. We may have missed five days in all those years.

That said, the specter of loss and the grieving that began over seven years ago are there. And although I don't allow myself to think much about it, I am also aware that the daily conversations are digging a trench of grief.

Such is the nature of love. There is no experiencing it without running the risk of loss. They are two sides of the same coin. So any description that I give of it will make it seem less organic than it really is. It will also run the risk of making the act of loving and grieving with someone sound like a laundry list of tasks to be completed.

I don't describe them here to give that impression. I outline them in order to be honest about the dimensions of grief and, hopefully, to name some of what we all face in loving and caring for one another. So, perhaps it's better to begin with an image.

**Think about grieving with someone as the act of holding someone in pain.** I say *holding* and not *hugging*, because hugging implies something that is done in a second or two. When we hold someone in pain, we can feel his or her body convulse. We can feel his or her tears, and we can also sense when he or she is trying to suppress the desire to cry. When you hold someone in pain, you can feel that person struggle to breathe. You can feel him or her flinch when the pain is at its sharpest. You can hear that person sigh with resignation. His or her struggle becomes transparent and visceral.

When we grieve with others, we hold them in the middle of their pain. We are touched by their vulnerability, and, because we all share the same vulnerability, it reminds us of our own—past, present, and future.

**What does that experience require, and where does it take us? First, we take the time needed to listen to and grieve with those we love.** We allow the kind of patient space that isn't marked by the thousand and one ticks that betray a lack of real love or squeamishness at having asked, "How are you?" We don't look away or check our phones. We don't discover someone to talk to who is more important or "less wounded" (the latter being words that reveal a lack of genuine love).

Yes, there are situations in which endless listening drifts into codependency, and all we do is provide someone a place to endlessly rehearse past losses. But that's not typically the problem. For most of us, learning to listen at all is really the challenge. Even the less difficult conversations are—more often than not—an exchange of soliloquies, each person saying what he or she had in mind, regardless of what the other party says. Patient listening acknowledges that we *don't* know what someone else is going through.

It is also important to bear in mind that what we hear can't be tracked against the backdrop of a "grief process." It was helpful progress when Elisabeth Kübler-Ross began analyzing "the stages" of grief, but it turns out that the experience of grief does not follow a map.[21] Denial, depression, anger, bargaining, acceptance, and a return to a meaningful life do not follow a lockstep pattern, and people who suffer loss return to various dimensions of the experience over time in ways that are not necessarily unhealthy.

**Second, we ask questions.** Not the kind of questions a gossip asks, which are full of prurient interest in gruesome details. Not accusatory and judgmental questions that imply that one suffers because he or she has done something wrong. To grieve with others is to ask questions that are organic to the information given to us, questions that are open-ended and invite any kind of answer that those who suffer might offer, questions that invite those who are in pain to name what they have lost and what it means to them to have lost it.

Questions of this kind never take the form of an interrogation. Instead they are born of compassion or the capacity to "suffer with," to patiently invite another human being to unravel the details of his or her journey. They invite those who suffer to elaborate, to express their feelings, and to voice their fears.

No two stories are alike. And regardless of the number of apparent similarities in our circumstances, every loss has an autobiographical character all its own. It is not enough to listen or to ask questions. The answers need to be heard and weighed in the way that those we love describe them. The experience is akin to walking through the most private rooms in a loved one's home. We suddenly discover small things that are arranged or cherished in unexpected ways.

I discovered, over time, by asking questions and by hearing how Dave answered them, that there was as much or more grief attached to losing the ability to practice medicine than there was to the actual prospect of dying. And the loss he experienced did not cover just the textbook definitions of what it means to lose a job. It touched on his sense of a life that was his and that had been carved out with effort and over time—a sanctuary in which he cared for others and was loved and respected for what he did.

Even as I try to describe what that loss meant to him, there is hardly a better description of it than to say that his work as a surgeon was one with what it meant to be himself; his was an identity wrapped up in a hundred and one experiences that were a part of his life narrative.

**Inevitably, grieving with someone we love entails opening ourselves to pain that is not ours.** For most of us, this is a huge spiritual, emotional, and cognitive shift. That's not surprising. Our culture has wired us to resist it. Our human nature co-conspires with our culture.

The modern life narrative is simple and unidimensional:

I have a right to be happy.

So, I work to be happy—as often as possible, for as long as possible.

When experiences rob me of that sense of happiness, it is because something is amiss.

So, I work to eliminate the obstacles to happiness as quickly as possible and return to the state of mind that is mine by right.

The roots of this mind-set run so deeply in us, that the notion that anyone would voluntarily step outside of oneself to embrace the grief of others is something we sometimes consider "sick" and "morbid." On the whole, we tend to think of grieving with others as a task we assign to professional caregivers who are both trained and paid to do it. The truth, however, is this: we can't care for others or truly love one another without surrendering the notion that happiness is our right or the goal of a life well lived.

**Sharing in the grief of others carries us by proxy into our own losses, past, present, and future.** That prospect alone keeps many people from ever walking with others through their grief. It is there, however, that something unexpected happens, if we are genuinely open to others. We discover that caring for those who grieve opens closed doors.

It introduces us to mysteries that cannot be discovered in any other way. Recognizing our shared mortality brings the realization that endings also shape the rest of our life's stories— that is, the end of a job, the end of health, the end of innocence, the end of life. We discover the mystery that in shouldering the grief of others, caring takes us out of ourselves. We will find renewed purpose, and our own grief takes on new balance and perspective.

**Along with those lessons, the experience of grieving with others teaches us things that even the professional literature often fails to grasp: we can't protect ourselves and shouldn't try.** The professional literature often misses these truths in large part because it is written for professionals and not for people who love one another.

To be sure, it is not wise to live with grief 24/7. Even those in its grasp are aware that they cannot live there constantly. Good grieving can involve laughter and stories. Being a surgeon and ex-Army, Dave was particularly fond of gallows humor. He also lived in Colorado for much of the year because, as he noted, "no one cares what you do for a living up here."

That said, to protect ourselves against grief—our own grief or that of others—is a mistake. If we focus on protecting ourselves from grief, we attenuate our love-journey with others, leaving them to make some of its hardest treks on their own. We live into an unreal version of life that is easily destroyed. And the massive self-protection that we practice leaves us without the resources for facing the hardest moments in our own lives—resources that grieving with others defines and sharpens.

Not the least of those life lessons for me has been Dave's courage and altruism. The treatments he has undergone have been part of a research protocol at Duke University's medical center. His experience has contributed to our knowledge of the disease that he is fighting. Regardless of the outcome, physicians will now have a better understanding of his cancer and new insights into its treatment.

**We also learn that grief is not a sign of faithlessness.** Grief is universal and has a hundred and one causes. It can be an indication that violence or great wrong has been done. It can follow on betrayal. It can be a sign of the world's broken and incomplete nature.

What matters is how we respond to our grief. For some that amounts to crafting the most positive response we can muster to life's losses. There is something to be said for sitting with one another and asking at life's frayed edges, "What's left? What's next?"

Some losses, however, are beyond retrieval; and, if what I have said here is true, there are losses that leave us without a lot of choices. It is here that Christian hope becomes important. We grieve, but we do not grieve like those who believe that life is over. It is not. We will live. Those we love will live. Our relationships with one another will endure and find healing. We will find peace and joy. What that will look like is hard to say. But imagine the best possible outcome and it will be better yet. In Christ, the most important dimensions of life are kept safe for us.

# QUESTION NINE:
## CAN I WALK WOUNDED?

# QUESTION NINE:
## CAN I WALK WOUNDED?

OUR GIFT TO THE WORLD IS COMPETENCE, OR SO WE think. Professionalism, continuous improvement, self-assessment, measurable outcomes, and certification are simply the latest terms in the arsenal of competence that is the modern way of life. So, we subdivide life into specialties, and when life is hard, we look for the appropriate expert. That approach has great gifts to life's hard places—attention and specialization among them.

**But...**

**Often what our suffering friends need most from us is an ability to confess our lack of control, acknowledge our own wounds, and then limp along beside them.** An ancient story from the Talmud underlines that need in picturing the Messiah:

A Rabbi asked Elijah, "When will the Messiah come?"
Elijah replied, "Go and ask him yourself."
"Where is he?"
"Sitting at the gates of the city."
"How shall I know him?"
"He is sitting among the poor covered with wounds." The others unbind all their wounds at the same time and then bind them up again. But he unbinds one at a time and binds it up again, saying to himself, "Perhaps I shall be needed; if so I must always be ready so as not to delay for a moment."[22]

According to the story, the Messiah is one who is wounded and shares in our vulnerabilities. His gift is not competence, and the story doesn't address that issue at all. He is other-directed. He treats his wounds, but he is not obsessed or preoccupied with them. The self-care that he practices is tempered by his availability to others. He also exposes his wounds one by one so that he is ready to help those in need. He is never completely wounded or exposed. The implication of the story is clear: success and competence have their place, but they are ultimately of limited value.

At the heart of Dave's small circle of devoted friends are two men who live like that. They are the most competent people I know. One is a clinical social worker, and the other is a cardiac anesthesiologist. They are also recovering alcoholics, and that has made all the difference in the way that they live their lives. Their experiences have pried competence away from them, and they no longer rely upon it. In fact, I think that they would both say that competence imperiled their spiritual lives, encouraging arrogance and selfishness. As a result, now they can walk with Dave in ways that share his vulnerability, even though the disease he is battling is radically different from the struggles that have bedeviled their lives.

Walking wounded does not involve living with your head down. It does not mean that Dave's friends talk in faintly tragic tones, that their conversations are thread through with whispered questions about his health, or that they talk constantly about how vulnerable they are.

**Walking wounded is about living in a completely and uncompromisingly honest fashion.** Dave's friends own their gifts and strengths. They also own their struggles and weaknesses. In one moment they have challenged Dave, recounted struggles of their own, and urged him to be honest about his struggle. In the next moment, they can tease him about the "cheap-ass" cars he drives.

The strength and quality of their friendship have taken the wounding that they have experienced as a given of their humanity, a given that they draw on without fanfare and something that they wear as easily as they wear the other aspects of their lives. And because they have paid attention to what that wounding has told them about the nature of life, they have learned a variety of lessons. They have learned to pay attention to life's spiritual dimension. They have learned to own their powerlessness. They have learned to admit that they need others. They have learned to love and let themselves be loved. More important, they have learned not to run from those lessons by hiding behind competence.

**That kind of vulnerability also makes it possible for them and for any of us to offer one another the gifts of friendship, redemptive possibility, perspective, and wisdom.** Relationships based upon competence turn our world into a place populated by experts, beneficiaries, and clinical transactions. Make an appointment, get some advice, pay a bill— that's the rhythm of modern life. *The ability to walk wounded creates the potential for something very different: friendship.*

By reintroducing us to one another as human beings who are capable of great strengths and great struggles, the transparency of walking wounded allows us to meet one another as we are. That kind of relationship doesn't require a contract or an appointment book. No one person does all of the giving. No one does all of the receiving. Everyone benefits from time spent together and the conversations had along the way.

I've become close friends with Dave's friends, and their relationships are clearly marked by mutuality. When we've talked about Dave, the conversations haven't been about his needs or even his illness. More often than not, they reflect with gratitude on the gift of Dave's friendship and the strength of his character. They have given to him, but he gives to them as well.

*Friendship of that kind opens up redemptive possibilities in which those who suffer or struggle not only find hope but also are often the ones who give others hope.*

Bob, one of Dave's friends, discovered the remains of a fighter jet that crashed in the Smoky Mountains years ago. The scattered pieces of the plane have washed down the hillside over the years, and Bob has retrieved them, fashioning crosses to wear for Dave and the "band of brothers" who have shared in Dave's journey. He notes that the creations not only are a reminder of their friendship but also symbolize the ability that God has to retrieve things of beauty even from the wreckage of our lives.

My friend Cheryl is a good example. Cheryl sat in her wheelchair Sunday after Sunday in the church I attended some years ago. She made her way to the sanctuary thanks to the efforts of her friends, and her presence there made a difference. Afflicted with ALS, or Lou Gehrig's disease, she was—in spite of it all—unfailingly hopeful, deeply interested in the comparatively minor struggles of her friends, and thoroughly in love with God and those around her. When I think of Cheryl, I remember her faith and courage. I am also reminded that there are always gifts that we can give to one another—regardless of the apparent limits and frustrations that slow us and seemingly confine us. Her smile, gentle touch, and sharp wit were constant sources of encouragement to me and to those who knew her.

*Such friendships not only open up redemptive possibilities like the ones I could see in Cheryl's life but also offer perspective.*

When my mother died over a decade ago, I found myself grappling with a new kind of loss, the nature of which I couldn't quite name. My friend David Lawson had lost both parents, and he had contemplated that loss at greater length.

David observed, "Fred, some of this loss is obvious to you, I am sure: the loss of your mother's companionship, the possibility of conversation. But another part of it is about a world forever changed by her death. In a sense our parents obscure life's horizons. They define our reality. But when they die, the horizons they obscured become visible to us, and we are forced to take ownership for a new reality. That process involves grief and learning."

David was right. Although his life circumstances were different, his willingness to walk wounded—his willingness to admit that he had been hurt by the loss of his parents—offered valuable perspective that not only helped me name my own loss but also offered a perspective I have been able to share with others.

Admittedly, there are times when we live too much out of our own perspective. We break in and say, "Oh, I know how you feel," in an effort to connect with one another and express solidarity. But walking wounded is clear about the difference between our own perspective and the perspective of those we love. In humility, it begins with the words, "in my experience." It is careful, in other words, to recognize that for each of us, life has an irreducibly autobiographical character; and no one's circumstances are an exact mirror or carry the same meaning as someone else's.

*Cumulatively conversations of that kind also craft a larger reality called wisdom.* We talk about wisdom as if it were an object, something out there, a thing to be found. But wisdom is, in fact, something crafted over time in friendship and community. It is the testing of perspectives against the realities of life. Wisdom is an evolving, growing creation that is one part worldview, one part a commitment to a set of values that arise out of that worldview, and one part the experience of testing that worldview and those commitments against lived realities of our lives. Wisdom is less about knowing "stuff" than it is about knowing what to make of the "stuff" you have learned and know.

The ragged edges of life—where we suffer and struggle—put those perspectives to their greatest and sometimes harshest test. The decision to walk wounded is, then, the resolve to craft a life marked by wisdom. If you go to the ragged edges of life, you will learn, not because suffering is a good thing, but because suffering tests the durability of our wisdom.

That is not a journey made alone. Dave has committed himself to that journey as he has fought his disease, and his friends have committed themselves to that journey by testing their wisdom alongside him. Each has brought his own worldviews and commitments to the journey. Over time all three of them have revealed where and how they have been wounded, what they have learned, and where they have struggled.

The result has been a body of wisdom that is larger than the wisdom that any one of them might have assembled alone. Dave has brought to their friendship the wisdom that arises out of a deep commitment to duty. Bob has brought the wisdom that arises out of careful listening and a wry sense of humor. Cliff has brought the wisdom that arises out of relentless honesty and an abandonment to love. As a result, all three of them have been forever changed and deepened in wisdom by the experience.

**That, perhaps, is why it is not just the Talmud, but the New Testament as well, that portrays the resurrected Jesus in the way it does at the end of the Gospels.** His wounds are still visible. He promises the disciples a greater intimacy than they have ever known. And in time, they will reflect on his wounding, just as surely as they reflect on their own. The disciples respond to his friendship, not because they are competent in unique ways—far from it, in fact. They respond with faithful resolve because they are finally able to walk wounded. It is worth remembering that the gifts of friendship, perspective, and wisdom are that easy to give. Just walk.

QUESTION TEN:
CAN I BE A FRIEND?

# QUESTION TEN:
## CAN I BE A FRIEND?

AS I THOUGHT ABOUT WHAT HAD BEEN HELPFUL TO my brother in grappling with his illness, it occurred to me that his friends possess five characteristics that make them people that he can rely on:

They *love* freely.

They acknowledge their own *mortality*.

They are *available*—to those in need, to God, and to themselves.

They are *vulnerable*.

They speak with *candor*.

Being a true friend to someone who is suffering is a journey, and, indeed, it may be summarized as a journey on which we develop those five capacities.

**As a prerequisite for caring for others the first character-istic—love—I suppose seems obvious enough.** To love is to care, and in order to care, we need to love—or so we assume. To care for someone at all requires a certain level of compassion and commitment.

But caring for those who suffer tests our deepest assumptions about the nature of love and our determination to love others. When we care for someone who suffers, the more superficial and emotional rewards of a relationship can quickly evaporate. It is easy to love someone who is young, vital, and strong. But fading strength and the smell of failing health can take their toll on loving feelings. The energy the caregiver pours out cannot always be returned in affirmation or gratitude.

A lot of people will tell you that they love you and will ask, "How are you doing?" But watch how quickly their interest fades when you begin to respond in any detail. Then the people who expressed all of that love begin to shift their weight. A certain kind of weariness creeps in around their eyes, and they begin to look beyond you, hoping that someone will show up and will derail the conversation. You can almost hear some people thinking like my friend at the cigar shop, "TMI—too much information. I'm sorry I asked."

A lot of people have said that they love my brother. Only a few have been willing to follow his struggle through two surgeries, weeks on end of radiation treatments, and the litany of side effects that follow on long-term chemotherapy. Are these people who just haven't learned to love? Or are they people who aren't confident enough to love through proverbial "thick and thin"?

There was a time when I was inclined to believe that people who mouthed loving words had just not learned how to care effectively for other people. I had little patience with them. That, however, is just the point.

*Real love, deep love only begins to take center stage when our commitment to others faces the test of life made hard and ugly.* It is work to learn to love beyond the platitudes. You can do it, but it is hard.

Dave's friends have not just said, "We love you." They have acted on their love. They have been there for surgery, hundreds of miles from home. They have had countless conversations over oceans of coffee. They have gone fishing with him and have spent hours on the target range. They have sat in hospital waiting rooms and with him in ICU for hours on end.

That kind of behavior lends content to the word *love*, spelling it out in concrete ways that fills hours and anchors days. Without that kind of real-life investment in him, the verbal wallpaper that many of us mistake for love would really mean very little.

Our eldest son, Andrew, is an Episcopal priest, and he and his wife live and work in the same city as we do, so we get to hear him preach from time to time. Not long ago, he talked about the parable of the Good Samaritan, and he made a telling point. Most of us believe that when the young lawyer asked Jesus, "Who is my neighbor?" that Jesus answered with this story in an effort to say, "everyone" is your neighbor. But, rightly, Andrew pointed out that Jesus doesn't actually answer the lawyer's question at all.[23]

Instead, he tells a story about a man who is beaten, stripped, robbed, and left for dead on the roadside *to whom only one of three travelers* (the priest, the Levite, and the Samaritan) *acts like a neighbor.* Andrew went on to say:

> The lawyer in the parable of the Good Samaritan wanted to know whom he needs to love. Jesus wants to know who is doing the loving. Neighbor is not a state of being but a state of action. Jesus is concerned not with the group of people who simply *are* our neighbors but with those people who are actually *being* neighbors. To be a neighbor means to make a decision to act; it's a choice, not a given.[24]

*The other dimension of love that proves important when people are suffering is respect.* For those who suffer, the most fragile commodity of all is a sense of worth, a sense of place in the world. Illness, divorce, unemployment, and death are isolating experiences that leave us feeling cut off from our surroundings, bereft of the connections that help us keep our bearings.

Love that is thread through with respect has a way of saying, "You belong. You are valuable. You possess worth, weight, and presence, and your suffering has not taken that away from you." By contrast, when respect is missing, love degenerates into pity or, in the more pejorative sense of the word, "charity." Then, even the activity that we associate with love matters very little.

In fact, love without respect is often patronizing and self-serving. As Robert Downey Jr. observes, someone who rides in and says, "Enough of this, I'll fix it," is simply indulging in "recovery vulturism."[25]

People who are well and prospering can ignore that kind of behavior. If you patronize them, they will tell you to "go to hell" and will look for better friends. People who are struggling don't necessarily have that kind of freedom.

If you've lost your job, in all likelihood you've also lost your sense of self-respect and control. If you are ill, you may feel sidelined and irrelevant. Regardless of the particulars, when life just plain sucks, we find it harder to name or ignore disrespect when it comes our way, and, for that reason, we are more likely to tolerate and internalize it. We don't get angry because we think it might be deserved.

By contrast, true love grounded in respect has the power to transcend, if not heal, some forms of suffering—not in the sense that love can guarantee physical recovery or a new job. Love is not magic. But love does have the power to move us beyond the impasse that suffering creates, grounding us in a larger sense of acceptance and security.

That may sound unrealistic, and, in the face of great physical and emotional pain, I completely understand the objection. However, our lives are always lived out within limits. Some of those limits go unnoticed for much of our lives. Other limits don't impinge upon our lives in a way that binds and hurts, or we adapt to them without noticing it. But, nonetheless, the limits are real.

Cognitive, physical, emotional, and social, such limits are there at every point in life. We live with less than perfect eyesight and hearing. We adapt to limited physical strength and chronic pain. The list is endless. The relationships that we forge with God and with other human beings make life possible in spite of those limitations. In fact, if we are at all healthy emotionally and spiritually, those relationships become the center of our lives.

**A second characteristic of Dave's friends is they acknowledge their own mortality.** In a sense, love isn't possible without some capacity for self-transcendence. If you are genuinely and actively devoted to the well-being of another person, then by definition you will be capable of getting out of your own skin. But to be present to someone who is suffering requires a capacity for self-transcendence that goes well beyond the norm. To walk with someone whose life has been shattered is not simply a matter of being interested in someone else.

When we walk with someone who is suffering we don't simply lay aside our own interests for a brief period of time. We put ourselves at peril. We surface our deepest fears. We expose ourselves to the dangers associated with those fears (abandonment, meaninglessness, the prospect of being overwhelmed, and the threat of extinction). And then, having faced those dangers, we must suspend the need to defend ourselves, so that we can hear, feel, taste, touch, see, and smell the fears of those we love.

This kind of self-transcendence is not simply a matter of moving beyond the boundaries of our lives to embrace the life of another human being. This is much more than "taking an interest in other people." This is the difficult, dangerous business of exposing our own fragile lives to the mortality that we know is a part of our own existence but that we don't want to acknowledge. To witness to another's pain is to say, "My circumstances don't force me to face this threat, but I am prepared to stand alongside you through the pain and fear."

Men, more than women, know how rare that kind of friend really is. Women are more often available to one another. For men, it is natural to wrap ourselves in the protective armor that distance and denial can give us. We talk endlessly and expectantly about the possibilities of life and about the things we will do one day. And, arguably, we ignore our mortality as a means of living.

However good or bad denial might be for us—and it has its uses—transcending our own lives to connect with others who are suffering makes it all but impossible to insulate ourselves from life's harsher realities. People who care step out of that sheltered place to stand with those who suffer. They face divorce, unemployment, disabling illness, lifelong impairment, discrimination, misery in countless forms, and—finally—death. For men, especially, this amounts to facing all of life's dragons at once.

Some of what others experience may never actually touch our lives. Not everyone experiences divorce or unemployment, for example. Some of it can't be avoided, like illness and death. And some of it will be all too real for us—reminding us of our own experiences from the past or struggles in the present. But true friends don't run those calculations. Instead they give the gift that Jesus described as the greatest gift we can give: the act of laying down our lives for the lives of others (John 15:13).

Among that rare breed of friends are those who will actually pay the full price: couples who cannot conceive who give their lives, their homes, and their fortunes to adopt children who have also suffered loss; crusaders who devote their life's blood to changing the behavior of a generation; and others who expend their life's fortunes and forego opportunities that would have made them wealthy, influential, or famous to work and stand with those trapped in misery. And, of course, there are those who literally die in the act of companioning others.

Some of them we know: William Wilberforce, for example, battled the slave trade his entire life, sacrificing the prayerful retreat he preferred to the political battles he was forced to fight on behalf of the enslaved. Mother Teresa lived among the poor all her life. More recently, Ambassador Christopher Stevens died standing alongside the people of Libya, and the men who stood alongside him were Glen Doherty and Sean Smith. Others, whom only a few will ever know, like my friend Stephen, who moved to Tanzania with the Peace Corps in order to teach math and engineering to people who might never enjoy the same educational opportunities he had been given.

The sacrifice does not need to be all consuming for it to be real. What matters is that we are willing to risk the possibility of death—be it physical, psychic, or spiritual. That is not just garden-variety love. That is self-transcending love.

Self-transcendence of this kind requires more than a mind-set, technique, or disposition. It requires spiritual and emotional maturity that sheds the countless defenses we rely upon in order to deny the truth of our inevitable demise. Instead, it demands that we live in a fashion that is alert to death's inevitability.

It is about realizing, in the words of Anthony de Mello, that we are "dead ahead"—the same wisdom that prompted Benedict of Nursia to urge his followers, "Keep death daily before your eyes."[26] Of course, awareness of that kind cannot be achieved without struggle, and it often begins with our own suffering.

In a previous book, *When Suffering Persists,* I shared this story.[27] In the winter of 1971, my high-school debate team managed to pry thirty dollars out of our principal's hands to attend an invitational debate tournament in Bardstown, Kentucky, south of suburban Louisville where I grew up.

It snowed that morning, the roads were slick, and in those days Kentucky's only answer to winter weather was spring. So, when we left Louisville for the tournament, the streets were still covered with snow. Somewhere on the narrow highway between the two cities, we fishtailed into a head-on collision with a two-and-a-half-ton truck.

I don't remember the collision. I do remember the results. Our twenty-something coach died en route to the hospital, all four of us on the team were hospitalized, and I emerged twenty-eight days later with a broken leg, a broken back, and a shattered arm.

That accident did not yield a sudden "foxhole conversion" or wholesale changes in my life. In fact, even at that point in my life I would have described myself as a Christian. But over a period of years, both our coach's death and my injuries did alter the way that I looked at life and life's choices, and at the heart of those choices was a newfound sense of my mortality.

I am not sure, for example, how patient I would have been with the struggles other people have if I had not learned from that experience. When you are the beneficiary of the care that other people give, and when you are deeply aware of how fragile your own strength is, you learn, if you are listening, to be attentive to the suffering of others.

The significance of that knowledge has grown over the years, and it does take time. We don't resist confronting the certainty of our death simply out of a fear that our biological lives will come to an end or because it brings us face-to-face with the unknown.

We resist that knowledge because admitting to the inevitability of our death is an "awakening" from sleep to the truth that "we are *alive*-facing-death."[28] That can be an unwelcome reckoning, and there is no easy path to accommodating it.

There are those who run from that knowledge for a lifetime. There are others who hide from it in addictions. And those are just two of the reasons that so few people are capable of the self-transcending love that embraces those for whom life is painful.

Even people whose professional lives are devoted to caring for those who suffer can and do run from their own mortality. I have met physicians whose choice of specialization was determined by that retreat. The objectifying language of medicine and, ironically, even palliative care (which is meant to look death in the eye) are, in fact, deeply informed by the denial of death.[29]

I have known clergy who confess that they don't visit nursing homes or hospitals because they "find them depressing." It is little wonder, then, that people who do not live in worlds or have professions in which they are supposed to care for the suffering and dying struggle with caring for those they love. The good news is that those same struggling people often prove to be the surprising exceptions as well.

How do we live into that self-transcendent knowledge of our own mortality, the knowledge that frees us to live with those who are "*alive*-facing-death?" There is, sadly, no formula. But there is wisdom on the subject to be had.

*One, sit with mortality when it makes itself felt.* One of the reasons that we learn so little from the reminders of our mortality is because we live in a culture that intuitively runs from the experience. Roughly speaking, the modern American mind-set revolves around the life philosophy: One, minimize the painful or unwelcome. Two, maximize the pleasant and satisfying. Three, if and when the painful or the unwelcome happens, run. Four, dispense with the painful or unwelcome experiences as quickly as possible and get back to feeling good.

In other words, our reaction to painful experiences—and, in particular, our reaction to death—is a bit like the reflexive reaction we have to momentary pain. We pull our hand back and move on to something else.

That makes sense when we are exposed to the possibility of physical injury. But when it comes to life's lessons, obeying that reflex short-circuits the learning process. The information that we are going to die is of a completely different order than an experience that threatens us with death. After the momentary adjustments it takes to avoid death, if possible, the realization that we might have died and that, inevitably, we will die is a valuable insight.

If you cannot sit patiently with your own mortality, it is all but impossible to sit with people who are in crisis. Their plight will seem unreal or short-lived. You will find it hard to care for them out of a sense of shared kinship. And your demonstration of love will be framed by impatience.

*Two, listen for the lessons that are all your own.* Sitting with our mortality never yields just one lesson, and no two lessons are exactly alike. We tend to believe that our ability to care for one another lies in connecting our experience with the experience of others. We can be helpful to others because we have experienced "their" grief, "their" illness, and "their" loss. "I know how you feel," we tell others.

Ironically, that is not the way it works. The words *I know how you feel* foreclose on feeling. Instead of being fully present to our own pain—never mind the struggle of others—we reduce that pain to an abstraction, a generic category, that is, illness, death, unemployment, and divorce.

The truth, of course, is that each of these experiences means something different to every one of us. And it takes time to unpack and unravel the significance of our own experience, never mind the struggles of someone else.

When we do the work of understanding our own experiences for ourselves, the result is not an encounter with the loss that everyone has had. The result is genuine empathy for the complexity of something experienced by someone else. That kind of empathy says, "Having plumbed the depths of my own struggle and having learned things I neither knew nor wanted to know about my own situation, I acknowledge that all I can do is witness to the complexity of your struggle, which I cannot understand."

*Three, give the lessons time to surface.* Life's deepest lessons are not learned all at once. Our most important lessons are likely to resurface over and over again in the course of our lives. Running from those struggles or checking them off of a list subverts our ability to grow. Like a bodybuilder who hopes to achieve physical goals with a few minutes in a gym once a month, if we hope for deep spiritual growth without the discipline of self-transcendence, we cannot hope to be present to our own suffering, never mind the suffering of others.

My friend Bill Davidson was a good example of someone who understood this. A child of privilege, he could have lived in relative ease. Instead, he lived a life of self-transcendence, studying medicine and then psychiatry, all the while battling illnesses that battered his body. Heart disease forced a traumatic bypass surgery. An error with a breathing tube made it difficult for him to speak and be heard. But none of that slowed his efforts to care for patients and friends. He still gave of himself.

Bill's approach is not the only one we can take to this spiritual discipline, but it is essential if we hope to be the kind of people who pass the Dave Test.

**Availability is the third characteristic.** Availability might have been discussed along with love, but it is important to highlight it. It is important in part because the word *love* is used so superficially. Far too often when we talk about love, we have little more in mind than sentimentality, a feeling, or affection. There is little more to our conversations about love than the affirmation that someone is essential to our happiness, a means to an end. Think about how it has become customary for friends, even male friends, to end a conversation by saying, "Love you. Bye." What does that sort of love mean?

It is also important to talk about availability because so many people who consider themselves loving aren't available at all. Some think that they love because they have the right politics or lend lip service to all the right causes. Some think that they love because they are in the right profession or write checks to charities. But being there for others when life sucks requires presence, an expression of God's love with skin on it. Those same "loving" people can have a really hard time when confronted with a friend in dire straits.

The Dave Test doesn't offer you the kind of caring that you can phone in, paper over with the right ideas, or deal with by writing a check. This kind of availability won't even necessarily look like love to the casual observer.

In the case of one of my brother's friends, he was a fellow physician who made himself available to travel thousands of miles by plane to be with Dave when he had surgery. He traveled first class because he has almost unimaginable back pain. When my brother was off having tests, my friend was outside the hospital smoking a cigarette, drinking a cup of coffee, and sitting with me. Both the jokes he told and the language he used would have made schoolgirls and more than a few adults blush. But he was there, boots on the ground, his heart wrapped around the trouble my brother was facing. He joked with my brother, evaluated what the physicians were telling him, and encouraged him when there seemed to be little in the way of encouragement to be had.

Why does availability matter so much? Availability is incarnational. It is hands-on. It is presence.

We cannot imagine our lives apart from the physical. The face you see in the mirror, the body you use to navigate the world, the places you've been, the trauma and joys you've experienced—they all have an inescapable, physical dimension to them.

A friend who is available to you when life sucks reminds you that the suffering you are experiencing has not cut you off from the rest of the world. That is why, even when we are dying, the touch of another person's hand can be such a source of comfort.

There are times when there is no substitute for being there: for being physically present, defenses down, and arms open.

**Vulnerability is the fourth characteristic of those who pass the Dave Test.** Thanks to a mixture of self-preservation, self-affirmation, denial, and cultural nonsense most of us live as if we never will die, get sick, divorce, lose a job, lose a child, or suffer abandonment. The reason my brother's friends mean so much to him is also because, as recovering alcoholics who have confronted their own demons, they are vulnerable enough to admit that they are, in fact, subject to the same losses and crises that others face.

It is one thing to walk alongside someone else (availability) and another to expose ourselves to reminders of our mortality by transcending our own needs (self-transcendence). But it is something entirely different to admit, "I am just as vulnerable as you are."

Whenever we walk with someone else through suffering, there are two ways that caring can go sideways. One way things can go wrong is to project our fears on someone else. We read so much of what we feel into the experience of another person that we assume that he or she is going through what we think that person is going through. That's almost never the case. Every unpleasant experience in life is just different enough from one person to the next to introduce elements that we don't necessarily share; or if we do, not all of the elements have the same significance. Losing someone to so-called natural causes is not the same thing as having a loved one commit suicide, for example. Losing a spouse is not the same thing as losing a friend. Each loss is unique because each situation is unique.

I've been there with friends who project their needs on others. You try to broach a conversation about something that hurts, and they tell you their story. Before it's all over you know far more about how they are hurting than you do about your own pain. Even if these friends get back around to making some tenuous connection to your own pain, you are pretty sure that you haven't been heard.

The other way things can go wrong is to walk with someone else as the resident expert. There is no friend like the resident expert, who is free of our flaws, always in control, and supremely calm. He or she knows what's wrong with you, knows where you've failed to understand what's wrong with you, and has a three-point plan for fixing things. That kind of person can spend hours with you but doesn't show a bit of vulnerability. Read the book of Job. Job had three friends like this. Job's friends knew why he had suffered, and so they never walked through his suffering with him or sat in the ashes he was sitting in.

It's not that resident experts aren't vulnerable like the rest of us. They are. They're just not aware of it, or they are trying damn hard to hide it, hence, the deep investment in demonstrating their competence. As long as they are in diagnostic mode, they don't need to examine their own struggles. They keep everyone at arm's length, if not off balance. But, then, resident experts aren't nearly as much help as they think they are.

When we play the resident expert game with other people, it really doesn't matter whether the advice we offer is sound or not. We are trying so hard to keep other people at arm's length that no one can really trust us, and we never really seem all that human. So, the advice that resident experts offer never seems all that accessible or useful.

Vulnerability is something completely different. It's not something you talk about or that you call attention to. It's about sharing or, more accurately, exposing our humanity in the company of people who suffer. Not in a weepy, self-invested way. This is not about some form of exhibitionism. It is about sharing our own vulnerability and that of another without rehearsing it, celebrating it, or telling long stories about how "we've been there" or how "we're scared, too." Those we care for can sense whether we are really vulnerable or not. Vulnerability is a reality that oozes out of the pores of our existence.

Another word for it that springs to mind is *authenticity*. But that word rings of Shakespeare's "be true to thyself," and that's not what I've sensed in Dave's relationship with his friends. What has made a difference to him is not that they live their lives with authenticity but that the lives they live are real. In other words, vulnerability is not about a life agenda and not about, "Look at me, I'm human, too." It's about being honestly, openly human in all of a human being's glory and strength, *as well as* in our brokenness and failings.

That comes through in the conversations Dave has with his friends. They are flesh and blood. They've had struggles and losses. They are aware that those losses aren't the same as the losses that Dave has suffered, and they don't pretend that they are. But they are on the same journey.

**Candor is the fifth characteristic of Dave's friends.** In our haste to help, it is often difficult to be honest. There are a lot of reasons, none of which necessarily have to do with ill will. We might be prompted to be less than candid with those who suffer in order to spare them some measure of pain or to avoid undercutting their will to survive. Love may seem like a strange motivation for lying, but when we care deeply about someone else, it is hard to say, "This is going to hurt like hell."

I haven't wanted to be honest with my brother about his illness, with friends and clients about the state of their marriages, or with people who are unemployed and looking for jobs where there are none and never will be. I have often wanted things to be better than they were or could be. Whenever I have hesitated, it's because I've been measuring the possible effect of my words. Sometimes "the right time" never comes, but the truth must still be lovingly told. My hesitation has not always been honest or helpful.

The trick is to finally say what needs to be said at "the right time." Rather than using "the right time" as an excuse to never tell the truth, Dave's friends have been honest with him. There are those who might argue that Dave's friends have been brutally honest. But telling a truth that we all share in, that we all sit with, and that we all discover together is different from truth as something we hand down from on high.

What I noticed about Dave's friends was that they discovered the truth along with him. They weren't there to "set him straight" or force him to "get with the program." They were there to scan the horizon with him, listen for the next challenge in his journey, and discover the hidden pitfalls.

"It is what it is," has become one of Dave's mantras over the years. But the way it is has been easier to accept because his friends have stood with him in the middle of that truth. This is the mark of those who pass the Dave Test. Can you stand with someone you love in the middle of the truth?

# POSTSCRIPT

*Monday, January 21, 2013*

THIS MORNING AT 2:00 A.M., I STOOD BY DAVE'S hospital bed and held his hand as he died. We were all there: Dave's wife, Belinda; his sons, Michael and Eric; Michael's wife, Beth; and my wife, Natalie. We watched and wept as first his respiration failed and then his heart. None of us had expected to be saying good-bye to Dave so soon.

When that last struggle was past we kissed him, told him good-bye one last time, and, finally, when we could avoid leaving no longer, we left. That night I said my last good-bye to my "little" brother.

On Wednesday, January 16, 2013, Dave went to the basement of his home to get a bit of fruit for dinner. None of us could have imagined how perilous that exercise of basic independence would prove to be. He made it down the steps, retrieved the fruit that he needed, and made his way back up the steps.

Somewhere along the way he tripped, suffered a seizure, or had a stroke. We will never know for sure what caused him to fall. What we do know is that he fell back down the steps, unable to break or slow his fall. His head struck the concrete floor behind him with so much force that the impact fractured his skull in several places, causing massive internal bleeding. The team that cared for him that night took him to the trauma center at Vanderbilt University Medical Center where the physicians and nurses did what they could to make him comfortable. After hours of silence, he rallied slightly on Friday, January 18.

He was aware that we were there. He responded to simple commands, squeezed our hands, gave us a thumbs-up sign, and smiled as much as anyone can smile around a ventilator. When they finally took out the ventilator, he could even say a few words.

"I love you, Dave."

"Love you, too, Fred."

"How are you doing, buddy?"

"I'm a wreck."

In classic OCD style, he even cautioned his wife and son to "be careful out there," as if there were any threat to compare with the one that swirled around him on that day.

But, in truth, the communication was fragmentary, disjointed, and brief. He could barely keep his eyes open, and none of the comments he made lasted long or were related to one another.

As his condition deteriorated late on Friday and still further on Saturday, January 19, he communicated with less and less frequency. His eyes remained firmly closed as if he was trying to muster the same inner strength that had brought him through two surgeries to remove parts of his brain. As though, with enough concentration, he could find his way out of this terrible place.

On Saturday, the words disappeared, and instead he mumbled incoherently. What we thought we heard him say that day probably had more to do with what we hoped to hear him say, than it did with what he might have been trying to say at all.

A long conversation with his physicians early on Sunday, January 20, led us to conclude that there was little hope of finding a comfortable, independent window of life between the countervailing challenges of his injury and the vagaries of his cancer. It was a long weekend of trying to be sure we weren't giving up and that we weren't clinging to a life Dave would not have wanted to live.

The decisions we made that day were very hard to make. We are all mortal. None of us lives forever, and we've known from the beginning that Dave's cancer was a death sentence. But loss is love's traveling companion, and to love deeply is to be hurt deeply.

Dave's own capacity for battling back also made it difficult to believe that he would not fight back again. He had two surgeries that I thought would condemn him to a largely sedentary life. Instead he sailed through them, as if to say, "Well that was a really unpleasant forty-eight hours. Let's get living again." In fact, just a week before his accident, he bounced back from a grand mal seizure that prompted one of his close friends to declare, "He's freaking Lazarus." It's an adjective I've never heard used in that connection, but it seemed to fit.

The Lazarus story is not a resurrection story, however, and this time even Dave's body seemed to be giving up the fight. So, we opted for hospice care and made arrangements to return him to his professional "home" at St. Thomas Hospital where he worked as a surgeon. There he would be surrounded by the friends and colleagues who had worked alongside him in helping others seven years ago, before the cancer took his career.

The choice was one that accorded with Dave's wishes—one we hoped would make it possible for him to die with a measure of dignity that would match the courage he had mustered to live his life, one that subordinated our needs to his, and one that trusted in authentic ways in the promise of the Resurrection.

That trip "home" was not to be.

At 12:30 a.m. on Monday, January 21, the nursing staff at Vanderbilt called to let us know that his breathing had changed and that there was not much time left. We drove to the hospital, sat with him through the little time that remained, held his hand, kissed his forehead, reminded him of our love, and prayed. At 2:05 a.m., he was gone.

Life is a journey of love and relationships. Caring for one another when life is hard strains and tests those relationships. We are easily tempted to run from its challenges—out of fear, out of selfishness, or out of a sense of inadequacy. To run from those hard places is to run from life itself.

Belinda and the boys had counted on more time with Dave. They wanted him there as husband and father. He was the anchor in their world. He had so wanted to see Eric graduate from medical school and to see Michael and Beth's first child.

I wanted him to be around, too. He was my brother. Our closeness had come too late in life, and I was as greedy as anyone for every minute.

What's more, I had just written the first two chapters of *The Dave Test* and was counting on his approval of the rest. He had read the completed chapters and said that they were true and honest. He did wonder if my editor would really let me say some of that stuff. I had been looking forward to having his responses on the rest of the book. I knew he would tell me when I was blowing smoke, using stained-glass language, or was just plain full of it. I hope the remaining chapters have been as true and honest in Dave's eyes as the first two were.

Dave and I talked twice a day for seven years—once in the morning and once in the evening. The hardest part of the days, weeks, months, and years ahead will be the silence.

Still, there is more than one kind of conversation, and love is not dependent upon audible conversation and voices. That does not mean that I believe Dave is alive because "he lives on in my heart." He does live in my heart. He also lives on in Cliff's heart and in Bob's heart, in the lives of his sons and his wife, and in the lives of those he touched and treated. But he is unrecoverably gone. His body will lay at Middle Tennessee State Veterans Cemetery. His spirit is with his Lord.

One day, however, we will all be gone. And if all we could rely upon were our memories of one another, then love and relationships would be a fragile gesture in a cold, endless vacuum. Love lives on because God wins and death cannot, because the Resurrection is not a metaphor for a "spiritual" transformation, but God's *no* to the counterclaims of death and decay.

I am blessed to have shared this journey with Dave. I love him, I am proud of him, and the grave cannot separate us. For that, I am utterly dependent upon the One who loves us both and am grateful in ways that escape expression.

But, oh, how I miss him.

Dave deep-sea fishing, 2006, after the first surgery.

# A CIRCLE OF FRIENDS

MY WIFE RIGHTLY NOTES THAT DAVE'S PARTING GIFTS
to me were the friendships that emerged or deepened over the
last seven years. Some of those friends were mine. Some were
his. But in one way or another, they were a part of this journey,
a circle of friends who gave of themselves.

In that regard, I owe a note of special thanks to friends Cliff
Emerson, Bob Reddig, David Schlafer, and John Ockels. Their
lives inspired much of what appears here, and some of them
read and commented on earlier versions of the manuscript for
the book. Above all, they have been the kind of friends who
would easily pass the Dave Test.

I would also like to thank my agent, Claudia Cross, at
Folio Literary; my editor at Abingdon Press, Lil Copan; Lauren
Winner, who worked tirelessly and patiently with me on

Abingdon's behalf; and Suzanne Austin, who assisted with preparing the final manuscript for publication. Their professional gifts, confidence, and patience have made all the difference in making *The Dave Test* available to a still larger circle of friends.

Finally, I want to thank my wife, Natalie, who loved Dave, too, supported me in my efforts to make this journey with him, and wanted to know on a daily basis, "So, how's Dave?" My soul friend and love, I am blessed to share life with you and am dependent upon your wisdom.

# NOTES

1. See Thomas Attig, *How We Grieve: Relearning the World* (New York: Oxford University Press, 1996), passim.

2. See Kelly Oliver, *Witnessing: Beyond Recognition* (Minneapolis: University of Minnesota Press, 2001).

3. Futurity.org, "In Social Isolation, Brain Makes Less Myelin," http://www.futurity.org/top-stories/in-social-isolation-brain-makes-less-myelin/.

4. Steve Knopper, "Marc Cohn Went Back to 1970 for Latest Album," *Chicago Tribune*, July 21, 2011, http://articles.chicagotribune.com/2011-07-21/entertainment/ct-ott-0722-marc-cohn-20110722_1_james-taylor-ray-charles-garfunkel.

5. The full lyrics can be viewed at http://marccohn.net/?page=song&album_id=23&song_id=293. Used by permission.

6. Elizabeth Lesser, *The New American Spirituality: A Seeker's Guide* (New York: Random House, 1999), 52. Lesser, director of the Omega Institute, describes "the new American spirituality" as a world in which each of us is our own best spiritual authority and invites her readers to

select (as I have already noted) from various practices to "string a neck-lace" all their own.

7. I have explored the way that we arrive at our religious and spiritual commitments elsewhere, describing it as "Triage Theology." See Frederick W. Schmidt, *What God Wants for Your Life: Finding Answers to the Deepest Questions* (San Francisco: HarperSanFrancisco, 2005), 31ff.

8. Gumby is the clay, humanoid creation of animation pioneer Arthur "Art" Clokey.

9. I owe this insight into the psalm to my wife, the Reverend Natalie B. Van Kirk.

10. See https://www.google.com/search?q=DEFINE+THEODICY&aq=f&oq=DEFINE+THEODICY&aqs=chrome.0.57j0l3j6212.5402&sourceid=chrome&ie=UTF-8.

11. Actually, the title is "Ac-Cent-Tchu-Ate the Positive." Lyrics are by Johnny Mercer, and music is by Harold Arlen, 1944.

12. G. K. Chesterton, *What's Wrong with the World* (New York: Cassell, 1910), chap. 5.

13. Frederick W. Schmidt, *When Suffering Persists* (Harrisburg, PA: Morehouse, 2001), 106–7.

14. Joan Didion, *The Year of Magical Thinking* (New York: Alfred A. Knopf, 2005), 32–33.

15. Friedrich Nietzsche, *Twilight of the Idols, or, How to Philosophize with a Hammer,* trans. Duncan Large (Oxford: Oxford University Press, 1998), 8.

16. See http://www.kellyclarkson.com/us/music/stronger.

17. At age twenty-four, Nietzsche was the youngest candidate ever to hold the chair of classical philology at the University of Basel. Appointed to the position in 1869, he resigned in the summer of 1879 because of health problems that dominated the whole of his adult life. He collapsed and suffered a mental breakdown in 1879 (possibly caused by tertiary syphilis) and spent the rest of his life under the care of, first, his mother and then, after her death in 1897, his sister. He died in 1900, and there is nothing about his life to prove the reliability of this not-so-biblical

maxim. See, for example, R. J. Hollingdales, *Nietzsche: The Man and His Philosophy* (New York: Cambridge University Press, 1965).

18. Schmidt, *What God Wants for Your Life,* chap. 2.

19. Harold Kushner, *When Bad Things Happen to Good People* (New York: Schocken Books, 2001).

20. Ralph Waldo Emerson, *The Essay on Self-Reliance* (East Aurora, NY: Roycrofters, 1908), 23.

21. Elisabeth Kübler-Ross, *On Death and Dying* (London: Routledge, 1969).

22. Sanhedrin 98a.

23. It is worth rereading the parable for yourself: Luke 10:25-37.

24. Andrew Van Kirk, "Go, Be a Neighbor," unpublished sermon, July 10-11, 2010.

25. Cal Fussman, "The Complete Robert Downey, Jr.," *Esquire,* May 2012, http://www.esquire.com/features/robert-downey-jr-intervention -2012#slide-6.

26. Saint Benedict of Nursia, *The Rule of St. Benedict,* IV.47.

27. Schmidt, *When Suffering Persists,* 1ff.

28. Michael Jinkins, *The Church Faces Death: Ecclesiology in a Post-Modern Context* (New York: Oxford University Press, 1999), 8.

29. Jeffrey P. Bishop, Phillip R. Rosemann, and Frederick W. Schmidt, "*Fides ancilla medicinae:* On the Ersatz Liturgy of Death in Biopsychosociospiritual Medicine," *The Heythrop Journal* 49, no. 1 (January 2008): 20–43.